Making a splash

A personal guide to networking

Rashmi Dubé

ISBN: 978-0-9955068-0-0

Dedicated to

Surya Kanta, Uma Jupiter

&

to all who make the decision to dive into the water.

Contents

Foreword

Dedicated to all who make the effort, believe in themselves and want to do better.

Thank you to my loves of my life: with particular gratitude to my mother Surya. Without her love and guidance and encouragement I would have never believed in myself.

What is 'Making a Splash' about?

As a lawyer[1], writing a book about networking is not the most obvious or natural thing for me to do. But, over the years, as an entrepreneur, lawyer and mediator, I have found networking to be crucial to my success and have, along the way, developed some tools to help me get the most out of it.

---

[1] The word lawyer is a general term and can mean anyone who gives legal advice. It is often used to describe solicitors, barristers, and others - more often than not it is used to describe the whole legal profession. The traditional legal profession in the UK is however divided into solicitors and barristers.

I am a solicitor and therefore advise clients and represent them on a day to day basis dealing with business advice. Outside the UK, the term solicitor is not recognised, the term lawyer is used instead. For this book I have used the term lawyer.

People often come up to me and say: "you make it look so easy. I find networking hard - can you give me some tips?" I have also given a number of talks on networking. The ironic thing is that I am really shy!

This is my personal perspective on networking. In this book, I share some of my networking experiences and offer my advice and tips on how to make it work for you. Hopefully, it will help you to improve your networking skills and your confidence, and eventually your network.

My focus is predominantly on face to face networking and building long term relationships. Of course there are other forms of networking including via social media and I have touched upon this in chapter 7 and included an article I wrote for London Economics on the art of digital networking in 2015[2].

For me, networking is more than just those formal get-togethers that are labelled 'networking events'. We all network all the time unconsciously, it is just not called networking. We meet up with friends, neighbours, sports team members. These are all part of our personal friendship and support network. I apply the same approach to formal networking as I do when building my personal relationships. The key thing is: be true to yourself - know your message, who you are and build valued relationships .

---

[2] See Appendix A, on page 134.

I have called the book 'Making a Splash: a personal guide to networking' because far too often a lot of us are outside our comfort zones when it comes to networking. It can be really scary meeting total strangers and talking to them with the aim of building a connection with them. It's like when we go swimming. The water's always really cold to start with. But by dipping our toe in to test the water we start to acclimatise to the temperature and it feels much easier to get in. We might even feel ready to dive in.

I hope that Making a splash will help those that are new to networking take the first few tentative steps and help those already networking to gain a few pointers and tips. The book is aimed at anyone looking to build relationships in their working arena.

Come on in – the water is lovely! Let's make a splash!

Chapter 1

Networking – it's all about relationships

"I actually love swimming but I just hate jumping in the water." Natalie Coughlin[3]

"If you want to learn to swim jump into the water. On dry land no frame of mind is ever going to help you." Bruce Lee[4]

Whether you're dipping your toe into networking for the first time or looking to improve your networking skills so you make a bigger splash, this book is for you.

I know that networking comes easy to some, but many find it really hard to do. It can feel really scary, walking into a

---

[3] An American competition swimmer and twelve-time Olympic medalist.

[4] A Hong Kong American martial artist, action film actor, martial arts instructor, philosopher, filmmaker, and the founder of Jeet Kune Do.

room full of strangers. It takes lots of courage to go up to someone you've never met before and introduce yourself. And what do you say anyway?

But I bet that of those people who are daunted by the idea of networking, most wouldn't think twice about talking to a stranger on a train or at the gym or at a friend's party. But that's networking too. And when you look at it like that, it becomes a whole lot easier.

As someone once said - you meet people for a reason, a season, or a lifetime. I believe that networking is an opportunity to meet people so that you can enrich their lives and they yours.

Definitions of networking

There are many definitions of networking. Some are simple, for instance: "to meet people with whom it might be useful to know, particularly in your job or business." (Dictionary.com)[5]

A more detailed definition is: "creating a group of acquaintances and associates and keeping it active through regular communication for mutual benefit. Networking is based on the question 'how can I help?' not 'what can I get?'" (BusinessDictionary.com). I have also heard people say: "informal networking can help further your career" and that networking helps you "to meet people who you will build a connection with and possibly form a relationship with".

---

[5] Definitions as of 2015.

I prefer the latter definition. The relationship is open ended, it can be business or personal.

For me, networking is, and always has been, about building relationships. In simple terms, you are building a web/network of people who have or will have some impact upon you and you upon them, whether in your private or professional life. Even more simply, it is about connecting with the people you like and who you want to help or support with the hope that they, in return, will help or support you.

What networking is not?

Networking is not the business equivalent of speed-dating! The objective is not to run around and meet as many people as possible. This is not a meet people marathon!

The objective is to build your network. The individuals you meet will form your contact database and some of these people will become your circle of associates/counsellors/advisors/referrers and friends.

Networking is NEVER about the SALE. Yes, you may have an objective, perhaps to get a new job, promotion or a new client. However, you are unlikely to get it from that first meeting or contact. People do business with people that they like and can speak to. You need to build a relationship of trust, expertise and delivery. This takes time. I met a gentleman some years ago at a corporate music festival in the local area through a firm of accountants. I stayed in contact with him over the years and as a result he introduced me to a group of people who have since become friends, including a lovely lady who also introduced me to another organisation that has asked to me speak about this book.

Some events that you attend such as conferences will have an educational element as well as networking which provide an ideal opportunity to build and develop those long term business relationships.

Remember that the person you're networking with might not need your services, but they might know someone who does. If you're just looking for the quick sale, you might ignore someone who could introduce you to lots of new opportunities. That's why it's much better to think of networking as a way to build valuable relationships rather than as a way to sell to people.

A lender in the financial world, for instance, may network sometimes with accountants. Their objective is not to make the accountant a client but to obtain referrals from the accountant who may have clients who are seeking access to finance. It is important that both parties have an understanding of what the other does and how they can add value to the relationship.

There are, of course, always exceptions to the rule:

As part of our services at Legatus Law, we offer business owners, managing directors and CEO's advice on commercial acquisitions and management buy outs. In 2013, I had just opened our London offices and was keen to build Legatus Law's profile in London. From my Yorkshire network of contacts, I learnt about an organisation that catered for our target market as well as those companies which were restructuring. With a little more research I discovered that there was a much-coveted London Ladies Lunch event. A perfect opportunity for me to network and raise our profile. I decided to go solo as it was my first attendance at the event, meaning I did not take a table of guests.

My first port of call at the event was to get to know the other people on the table. As a result, I got talking to a lady who was an insolvency practitioner. The perfect start! We chatted for a bit, getting to know each other and discussing what we both did.

As the event continued, I went to each table where I knew at least one person to say hello to. My aim was to see if that person could introduce me to someone I did not know at their table — this is also a good way to catch up with people that you might otherwise have to spend time arranging to meet for a coffee. Towards the end of the event, the lovely lady who I'd met earlier came bounding towards me, grabbed me and said, "I need to introduce you to someone".

She introduced me to a gentleman[6], himself an insolvency practitioner, who was at that moment looking for a firm to work with on construction recovery. We got instructed the following week!

Things don't normally happen quite as quickly as that, but of course it wouldn't have happened at all if I hadn't:

1. Been at the event - if you're not present, you can't meet people who just might be key to your success.

2. Developed a relationship with the lady at the table. It would have been very easy for me to simply wander off to speak to people I already knew. But I made the effort to speak to someone new.

3. Clearly explained my message - it was important that I got across who I was and the work my firm did. My new contact was then able to introduce me to exactly the right person!

I still have very good relationships with both parties. Getting to know people can allow you and them to open doors for one another.

Luckily nowadays there are a lot of organisations that say "turn up for the event but no selling". This is great! It allows you to get to know people without any form of pressure. I highly recommend going to these events so you can get a feel for speaking with people for no other purpose than to

---

[6] At this particular ladies lunch gentlemen were also invited as guests.

see if you can perhaps offer them some kind of assistance.

The 'no-selling' rule is true both at group events and on a one-to-one basis. Having a coffee with someone is still networking as it is during these sessions that you can really get to know someone. Often, when you take someone for coffee, they already have some knowledge and understanding of your experience and expertise, from what you have told them already. Now, they want to know about who you are in more detail. For example, when someone meets me, they usually already know that I am a lawyer who specialises in business law, contracts, disputes, and mediation. They are also likely to know that Legatus Law works with businesses on day to day activities like drafting contracts and agreements, on the commercial/corporate aspect of their business, dealing with disputes and helping with restructuring if required. The coffee meeting means I can expand on how Legatus Law and I can help their business. But, more importantly, it means I can find out what their business does and more about the person I am meeting. Yes, of course, I want to see if we can be instructed in a new matter and convert the person into a new client but that is not my only or primary objective. First, and foremost, I want to find out how we can help each other and build that relationship.

Men and women - do they network differently?

Is there a gender difference when it comes to networking? A

lot has been said about gender differences over the years and how gender affects how we approach a variety of issues. I look at this in a little more detail in chapter 8.

There is often a lot said about the 'boys' network'. Men always seem to network with men or pass work between themselves. It can be hard for women to infiltrate their 'organisation' or group. It is claimed that this is likely to stem from the 'bonding' that men do. They get to know each other on the golf course, in the pub or going to rugby games or football matches, all of which women may be excluded from. Plus, men have traditionally just networked with their colleagues who historically have been men.

But the landscape of networking is changing. If we take an overview of Fortune 500 Board Seats held by women - in 1995, it was 9.6%; in 2005, it went to 14.7%; and by 2010 it was 16.9%[7].

Of course, some people may struggle to adapt to this change. If you've always networked in a particular way, it can be difficult to adjust. My advice: find what works for you but keep an open mind, maybe even try something new. You may just like it!

RR – Rashmi's Rules on networking

These are the rules I follow when networking. I am not saying that knowing them is the golden ticket – but they

---

[7] www.catalyst.org - statistical overview of women in the workplace as per September 2015.

work for me and might give you some guidelines that help you to develop your own rules.

1. Know yourself and your message

2. Be prepared

3. Listen

4. Follow up.

To help you get to know yourself and the message you want to get across when networking (topics I cover later in the book), you may find it helpful to make a list of your current views on networking. How do you feel about networking? What aspects of networking are you good at and what elements do you struggle with? You may then want to write something under the headings below. I have populated it with some examples get you started.

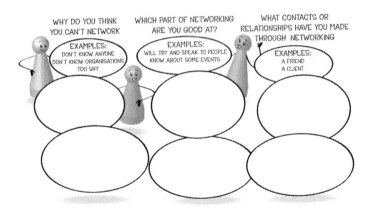

If you are going swimming you may want to wear a swimsuit

What type of swimsuit do you like to wear? Does it depend on whether you are going to the swimming pool to exercise or to the beach to have a dip in the sea? One size does not fit all and neither can one outfit (whether that's a full swimsuit, shorts, bikini, or speedos) suit every occasion. It is important to understand who you are. It is easy to write this but very difficult to put it into practice. What we should always remember is that we are constantly evolving and changing and so will the image of who we are.

I am a lawyer and mediator who has worked in the commercial/corporate, civil litigation arena and then in construction and engineering law. When the recession hit the UK in 2008/2009, statistics from previous recessions indicated that insolvency and debt recovery had a proven track record of success during a recession. It was a good and profitable business to have, helping business owners recover their debts. So I established a new company called Liquid Recovery to carry out debt recovery work. I had to get our new message out into the market and the branding and image of Liquid Recovery was a vital part of this. I have always thought colours are important in how you present yourself so, at the time, I wore a lot of turquoise as that was the colour for Liquid Recovery.

A few years later, when I opened Legatus Law – a law firm

that catered for owner-managed businesses' legal requirements, the message changed dramatically as did the image and the branding. Legatus Law's message was that we were protecting businesses and their directors and shareholders, and the colours changed to red and gold. What I had not appreciated and am still finding out today is how well I had got my message out in the time of Liquid Recovery. In the first year of Legatus Law I would meet people that I have known for a long time and they still didn't understand that I had changed firms. I addressed this and ensured that my message in the market was clear – I was someone who had been in the legal industry since 1997! My brand works now, so it's good news, not a complete loss! But it is important to realise that it's not easy to get your message across. And if you change horses mid race, people will get confused with your message.

This was not the first time this had happened. In the early 2000's I decided I wanted to study construction and engineering law, to add to my expertise in commercial law and litigation. I was in a new arena with new people – and had to work really hard to let the market know I had a new dimension to my offer. When I qualified as a mediator in 2009, I again had to consider how to get this message out. It is important to understand who the message is going to and for what purpose. For instance, in terms of mediation I needed to communicate my message to other lawyers, solicitors and barristers predominantly.

Knowing what you want from networking

You need to understand what it is you want to say to others about yourself personally, and about the business or company you represent (whether you're an employee, manager, director or stakeholder). You also need to think about what it is you want to achieve from networking. What is it you are looking for on a fundamental level? Don't forget it can be as simple as attending an event to hear the speaker.

If you are new to the industry, a graduate or new to the working environment - it may be that you just want to get to know and introduce yourself to the players in your arena. This is also a good way to build your confidence and get to know yourself better.

Networking from my perspective is simply getting to know the people in your environment. If you work in a large organisation, this will include your fellow employees. But this is not just about your work life, where you can network both internal and externally, but also about your personal life. It is how we make friends from the relationships we build. Working life is just as important, enjoy what you do and enjoy the relationships you build with other people. Over the years, I have met some amazing people and made wonderful friends.

Happy networking!

I have always liked the title of one of Sir Richard Branson's[8] books - "*screw it, let's do it.*"

"*If you haven't found it yet, keep looking. Don't settle. As with all matters of the heart, you'll know when you find it. And, like any great relationship, it just gets better and better as the years roll on.*" Steve Jobs[9]

---

[8] Sir Richard Charles Nicholas Branson is an English business magnate, investor, and philanthropist. He is best known as the founder of Virgin Group.

[9] An American information technology entrepreneur and inventor. He was the co-founder, chairman, and chief executive officer of Apple Inc.

Chapter 2

Know yourself

"*I love swimming in the open sea but am equally happy in the pool.*" Rashmi Dubé

"*Believe in yourself, not only in swimming, but in life itself. You always have to have fun. You have to have an open mind. If you're not enjoying it, don't do it. Life's too short.*" Debbie Meyer[10]

"*Everyone has the right to run his own life - even if you're heading for a crash. What I'm against is blind flying.*" Mae West[11]

---

[10] An American former competition swimmer, a three-time Olympic champion, and a former world record-holder in four events.

[11] An American actress, singer, playwright, screenwriter, whose entertainment career spanned seven decades. She was one of the first artists to understand both business and personal branding in her industry.

I recall getting some public speaking training and coaching from Red Voice's Victoria Pritchard and, at the time, Helen West. During the session I said that I wanted to start my talk with a joke or maybe tell one during it. I had seen other presenters using this approach and it always appeared to me to warm the room. However, Victoria made it very clear to me that I was "not funny." What? I'm not the next Peter Kay or Catherine Tate, of course not! But really how hard can it be to tell a joke and have the audience 'warm' to you? Victoria explained to me that my talk was formal and structured and in fact people were not expecting or wanting to have a joke. "Rashmi," she advised, "you are just not funny, keep it simple".

I needed to understand what my message was, and to know myself in the context of public speaking, which was quite different from the 'networking Rashmi'. The brand was the same, the message was the same, but the delivery needed to be quite different. The relationship I was building during the presentation was very different from the relationship I build with people on a one-to-one basis.

Knowing yourself

I know who I am when I network. It is very close to who I am in my personal life but not identical. I am not saying that I am misleading in any way. My core values of decency, honesty and wanting to help others remain the same. My personality is still bubbly, friendly and smiley. That is my core persona whether in work or in my private life.

However networking is not simple, particularly if you lack confidence or the ability to be social. It requires a level of confidence and self-belief. Not all of us possess these qualities naturally. Sometimes, you have to take on a slightly different persona to help give you the confidence you need.

It's important to know yourself - know what your personality is and what your core values are - at a fundamental level. That way, you can start to build a networking persona that complements and enhances the person you are in your private life.

Let me explain.

I have, from an early age, been fairly confident and comfortable in my skin. This was not a natural thing. It was something I learned having travelled at the age of 11, to Des Moines, Iowa, in the USA Before that, I was a very shy, introverted girl, which is still my default position. When we moved to the U.S I not only had to learn to talk to people and make new friends, I also had to learn to adapt to a new culture and new ways of doing things. It was not easy. In fact it was very difficult for an extremely shy young girl to leave Woodley, a small suburb of Reading, Berkshire, UK, where she had lived most of her young life, to move to a new country with no friends and no barometer of what was acceptable socially and what was considered 'geeky'. There were social rules and as young children we apply pressure upon ourselves to fit in. Self-doubt kicks in as we question ourselves, "what happens if they don't like me?", "what happens if I don't make friends?"[12]. It was a scary time and I was very bad at it. I did not have a clue.

I was, metaphorically, pushed into the swimming pool, fully clothed, unprepared. I was hit by that first wave of cold water when you gasp for air before your brain kicks in and says "you need to swim". I faced a choice: should I swim up to these new people and see what happens or should I hold on to the side and watch? The problem with the latter is that you might feel safer, but you will also feel cold because you are stationary. The truth is you will feel a lot warmer once you start swimming, once you start joining in. What if you don't know how to swim? Grab some armbands and start learning!

So that's what I did (after holding on to the side of the pool for a short period of time!).

I persisted through elementary school, junior high and high school learning to, essentially, network. When I came back home to England all I had to do was fine-tune my newly-acquired skills for the English culture. The greatest things I learnt during this time of my life were:

---

[12] Oddly I find that we are somewhat 'back to school' with social media – how many "likes" does one have, how many friends, or how many connections? I personally think it is quality not quantity that's important. Some things are posted for future generations to read and learn from, not everything has to be about the here and now. Not everything has to be about one's self, some things can be about the community in which we live in and how we can help one another within that network.

- Never be afraid to try anything or speak to people

- My fear was my biggest block

- People are generally nice

- Always be present and have a positive energy and outlook

- Believe in yourself and what you are doing.

I'm sure, like me, that your experiences in life have helped to define who you are. We adapt and change as we grow older and as we do we get a better idea of who we really are. My experiences increased my confidence and helped me develop my social skills, but I remain, at heart, that shy little girl. It's what I call the default position - the person you will always default to when you're in a difficult situation. Sometimes, when I'm networking, I do not feel bright, bubbly and smiley; sometimes I am tired or just plain nervous about the room I have entered.

This happened recently when I was invited to a public appointments talk at the Royal Armouries in Leeds, West Yorkshire, England. I've become so used to walking into a room and knowing most of the people in it. But this time I could not see anyone I knew and immediately felt really nervous, defaulting back to the shy person I once was. I was once again hit by the coldness of that first jump into the pool when you have not yet acclimatised to the water. So, with nerves and self-doubt setting in, what did I do?

(False) confidence

Sometimes, for one reason or another, you might not be feeling particularly confident ahead of a networking event, so you need to find a way to create false confidence. One way might be to have a topic of conversation to fall back on. For example, I once spoke to a gentleman who told me that he has always been shy and before any networking event or meeting he had to draw on the techniques he has learnt to help him though the process. So when he was first introduced to me he was very uneasy and nervous, although I did not notice. As I am pretty relaxed in my approach and allow people to explore a variety of topics, we finally hit upon a mutual topic of conversation – our love for cricket. This allowed him to start talking and relax.

Even if you are usually a confident person, there may be times when you are just not in the mood for socialising or networking. Perhaps you've had a hard day at work or other things are happening in your personal life and a networking session is the last place you want to be. But you have promised people that you will attend an event, and it's important to keep that promise.

In these instances, it's nice to have a character you can adopt who makes you feel more confident. While most people are friendly when they turn up at a business event (because if you are miserable or unpleasant then nobody will want to talk to you!), having a character to draw upon can give you a real confidence boost. A lot of people do this. Take Beyoncé[13] for instance. She creates a character called Sasha Fierce for when she performs. She openly admits that when she sees herself on the TV, she says, "who is that girl? That's not me, I wouldn't dare do that."[14]. She's created a character to enable her to perform. Fictional characters such as Wonder Woman and Superman created alter egos to be able to participate in another world. Superman created Clark Kent to be accepted by, and network with, people in the newspaper world. The Clark Kent persona is almost completely different to Superman – he is very quiet, shy and always portrayed as physically weak compared to the stronger superhero Superman but they both have the same core values which never change. Decency, honesty and a love of helping others are values present in both characters.

That's how it works you are still the same person, you just create a persona to help you get through whatever occasion or challenge you have in front of you. I call it false confidence, but in actual fact there is nothing false about it. The confidence is within us, we simply muster it up, believe it to be false in order to get through a situation but in reality we always had it to begin with. It's like how the hardest part about swimming is the initial entry into the water. Once

---

[13] Beyoncé Giselle Knowles-Carter is an American singer, songwriter, record producer and actress.

[14] Interview with Beyoncé - 'Illuminati: Beyoncé is dead. I am Sasha Fierce' on YouTube, September 2003.

you're in, the current will take you some of the way with very little effort.

It took me a while to work out who my character/persona/ alter ego was. Who could I draw on when I was lacking in confidence or nervous? In the end, I chose not just one person but a combination of people including Mae West, Bette Davis[15], my mother[16], HRH The Queen[17], Indira Gandhi[18], Madonna[19], Oprah Winfrey[20] and Mother Teresa[21].

These women are or were all strong, have had to communicate and network with people to obtain their positions or goals and had to have the belief and confidence

---

[15] Ruth Elizabeth 'Bette' Davis was an American actress of film, television and theatre. Regarded as one of the greatest actresses in Hollywood history.

[16] My mother - a lady who taught me a lot about relationship building and who has always been an inspiration to me and others she meets. A nurse by profession who believes in helping and guiding others whenever and wherever possible.

[17] HRH The Queen of the United Kingdom, Canada, Australia, and New Zealand, and Head of the Commonwealth. Regardless of whether you are a royalist, you have to appreciate that networking would be a large part of her royal duties.

[18] Indira Priyadarshini Gandhi was a key 20th-century stateswoman, a central figure of the Indian National Congress party, and to date the only female Prime Minister of India.

[19] Madonna Louise Ciccone is an American singer, songwriter, actress, and businesswoman. She has constantly changed her image and message within the industry moving from singer to new arenas of film and business.

[20] Oprah Gail Winfrey is an American media proprietor, talk show host, actress, producer and philanthropist.

[21] Mother Teresa, also known as Blessed Teresa of Calcutta, MC, was a Roman Catholic religious sister and missionary. Through her networking and reaching out to people she changed the world.

to do it. They are always knowledgeable in their own arenas and dressed for their personal brand. Madonna is a great example of being consistent in terms of her message – her look changes all the time, but her personal brand as musical performer and businesswoman remains consistent.

Choosing a fall back character is just one of the tools you can develop to help you get through a networking event and develop those vital relationships. When I attended the Royal Armouries public appointments event, I felt way out of my comfort zone, like I'd been pushed overboard in the middle of the ocean! So I quickly drew on the characters that, for me, represent people who are strong, always dressed for the occasion and who know how to turn it on when the moment requires it - Bette Davis and my mother. For the first 20 minutes or so, I took on those personas to help get me through the door, into the room, approach an open group[22] of people, introduce myself and start to chat to people. I sometimes see my characters as armour. I feel protected by them a little bit like Linus from *Peanuts*[23] carrying his blanket everywhere he goes! I was still my smiley, bubbly and friendly self but with my comfort blanket of personas.

It was still really hard because I did not know anybody, or least could not see the few people I did know in the room. It became easier once I ran into someone I knew who then

---

[22] See Chapter 5.

[23] *Peanuts* is a syndicated daily and Sunday American comic strip written and illustrated by Charles M. Schulz.

introduced me to several other people. At that point, I was able to ease myself a little more into the networking and not lean on my false confidence as much.

In reality there is no difference between going up to speak to strangers or having someone I know introduce me to strangers, but having someone you know there offers comfort, like armbands when you are swimming in what feels like the ocean! Later I was introduced to a lovely lady who helped me understand her role as a trustee at the Royal Armouries. That led to a coffee and a very lovely new friend in my life.

Choosing a character

Choose a character that works for you and that you feel comfortable with. Your 'go to' person should be someone that you identify with and could be a fictional character, a celebrity, a persona you create, or a person you know. One contact of mine, for example, uses her first boss because she was a very strong woman, who always had a solution to a problem. You could have a variety of people that you like in your head so you can call on the right one, depending on the situation. You might get inspiration from graphic novels, television characters, actors, writers, presenters, models or people in your everyday life like parents, partners or siblings. Inspiration is all around us we just need to become aware of it and tap into it.

After all, we adopt different personas in different situations in our private lives too. If something positive happens, it can make you light up and act in a more happy-go-lucky way or, if you're going through a traumatic time, you can pull on strength that you didn't even know you had, yet you're still the same core person.

As Rashmi Dubé, I have many parts to play: the daughter, the sister, the team player in sports, the lawyer to the client, the lawyer in front of the Judge, the lawyer when negotiating with the opponent, the mediator for lawyers and their clients, the employer, the entrepreneur, the networker, the mentor, the speaker, the friend, and the charity volunteer. I am sure you too will have many parts you play: parent, spouse, student, graduate, and employee, head of department, business partner, director, CEO, or trustee to a charity. These different roles are all variations of who we are, finely tuned and constantly developing. Of course, like with everything in life, you will keep changing and evolving. At the moment, these personas suit who I am but it doesn't mean I won't change them or bring in new characters at a later date.

On the next page, list characters and characteristics that suit you and how you see yourself wanting to be in a networking environment. To help with this, think about how you act with your friends or family and how at ease you are with them.

Remember, it may be worth reviewing this chart from time to time as your comfort zone widens.

CHARACTER & CHARACTERISTICS

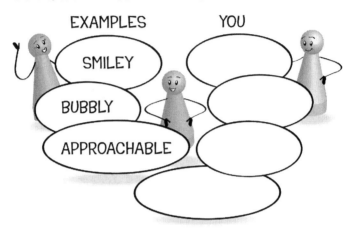

EXAMPLES   YOU

SMILEY

BUBBLY

APPROACHABLE

Chapter 3

Personal appearance & message

"*Only when the tide goes out do you discover who's been swimming naked.*" Warren Buffett[24]

"*Appearance matters a great deal because you can often tell a lot about people by looking at how they present themselves.*" Lemony Snicket, The Miserable Mill[25]

Everyone that you meet in business has developed an image for themselves, whether intentionally or not. Some people go as far as creating a specific look, such as the way they

---

[24] An American business magnate, investor and philanthropist. He is the most successful investor in the world.

[25] *The Miserable Mill* is the fourth novel of the children's novel series *A Series of Unfortunate Events* by the author known as Lemony Snicket.

trim their moustache, wearing red kickers, wearing a three-piece suit with a spotted handkerchief or simply adding an attractive brooch to their outfit.

Personally, I like to wear red. That's because it is the brand colour of Legatus Law. I chose the exact red I wanted - a distinctive, strong and deep red - because that's the impression I want to give the people I meet - that I and Legatus Law are distinctive, strong and dynamic. Don't get me wrong – I don't wear red all the time but where I can I will.

Personal brand

What do I mean by personal brand?[26] It is how you present yourself to others. The impression you want to leave on others. Wikipedia describes personal branding as "the ongoing process of establishing a prescribed image or impression in the mind of others about an individual, group or organization."[27] Sometimes, of course, people get a different impression from the one you intend to give. For instance, you might want to be seen as reliable, but because you're often late to appointments, the people you meet view you somewhat differently! Remember, part of your personal branding is in the eye of the beholder.

---

[26] There are experts on building personal brands but for this book I am considering your brand in terms of appearance and message for networking purposes only.

[27] Wikipedia encyclopaedia dated 24 May 2015.

Clearly, the first step in developing your personal brand is working out what you want to say about yourself. Also you'll need to consider how your personal brand relates to the brand of the company you work for or represent.

Personal appearance

What message do you want your appearance to convey to your audience? Some people, for instance, choose to associate themselves with 1940s clothing or make up to make themselves stand out. Sport teams have a similar approach. Look at football teams when they are not playing - most teams nowadays when travelling to and from matches wear suits with ties in the team colours. Whilst playing, some rugby teams go as far as ensuring all players wear the same colour shoes. The message is clear - this is who we are and we are a team, and it's all said through their attire.

It is very different for men and women. Men have less to play with. If you're a man and you're wearing a suit then maybe you can bring something different into your image through your tie or other accessories. I know someone who has always worn a purple handkerchief in his breast pocket, regardless of the company that he worked for - it was his personal branding. It's small things like that which you can just add to your outfit which will help people to remember you and make you stand out from a crowd of other men in suits. Or simply, in some cases, people get to know that you will always turn up smartly dressed.

Spend some time considering your appearance and personal brand and that of your company. Your personal brand will develop over time and change as you change as a person.

My personal brand extends to my accessories and my shop window, which is my business card. I find in most parts of the world when I hand over my business cards I get what I call the *American Psycho* moment: The film (2002, directed by Mary Harron) has a scene where the main character, Patrick Bateman, is given a business card and the whole time he is thinking of the thickness, colour and watermark of that card. People comment on the thickness of Legatus Law's business card, the colour and the foil. It stands for what Legatus Law is - a cut above the rest, a strong firm that is dependable and delivers quality. This is the firm's brand which goes hand-in-hand with my personal brand when networking.

So it is important to understand:

- Your brand: what is it you are trying to convey to others about who you are?

- What is your message?

- What is your appearance? How does it reflect your brand?

Deciding on your personal image

In terms of appearance, there are a variety of options which depend on your sector and the event you are attending. If you're an undergraduate or a worker in your early twenties, the look will be different from someone in their 30's, 40's, 50's or 60's. However, if you don't entirely know or understand yourself or what it is you are trying to say to others you can end up sending out mixed messages. As you mature, you start to get a clearer picture about yourself, often through other people's input. For example, I've been through some tough times in my life and somebody at my book club once said to me: "You're an amazingly strong woman aren't you? Look at what you've achieved." I was stunned by that comment. You don't always realise just how you come across until someone points it out – it can be hard for us to recognise. We therefore can be appear to be strong and confident but inside be shaking like a leaf.

Take a look at your own personality traits. This helped me in understanding that I can use bold colours, because that is who I am. I am bold when it comes to the law, I tackle things head on and have a creative approach to resolving issues. As you mature you will understand what works for you and what you like; you slowly become more comfortable in what you choose to wear. What I would say is I always reassess the image and ensure that I am in line with what it is I want to say (and, whether I am age-appropriate - oh dear, that comes with age!). It is like giving the wardrobe a spring clean.

For me, the image I want to portray depends on the kind of event I'm at. For example:

- If I'm in court, I will wear a dark suit and keep to what are known as 'court colours' in the traditional sense as I am a traditionalist.

- If I'm making a speech at an event then I will wear an outfit that is in line with my branding or the event; my preference would be my brand colours, preferably red. Importantly I wear what I feel confident in on the day.

- If I'm a guest speaker at a university then I don't tend to wear a suit jacket, I'll wear a cardigan and will decide on the use of colours on the day. I want to be more approachable to my audience.

- If I'm doing a presentation or a pitch for a new client I will wear what is generally expected of a lawyer or a mediator. That makes me feel comfortable with the potential new client.

- At networking events – people are expecting to see a lawyer, someone who is an expert in their field so I will dress accordingly. So, either a suit or a dress and jacket and sometimes in my corporate colours if it's a formal day event.

- If a company has invited me for the day to an event, a more relaxed look could work.

- Black tie evening events are great for men – you really cannot go wrong whether a traditional black tie or kilt, except maybe by dressing all in white when the occasion does not call for it. For women, it is more complicated - how low, how short, what colour, do I feel comfortable? It comes down to personal judgment. Don't be afraid of using colour.

If you are unsure about what to wear for an event, ask somebody – particularly if they have been to a similar event before so they know what is appropriate.

The image does not stop at clothes but extends to shoes, hair and nails. A good manicure (men and women) always helps. There are two examples I would like to share with you. The first is a magician. When he performs magic on a one-to-one basis, he is aware that his audience is looking at him the whole time so he has to make a decision about his appearance. This includes the need to have regular manicures because his audience is constantly looking at his hands when he performs card tricks, for example. Another example is a lovely lady I know who worked for a number of years with a financial institution. Although very well-known, she was predominantly behind the scenes. She subsequently got a new position that involved a lot of networking and being seen by the industry. Almost overnight, her wardrobe, hair and overall appearance transformed. She knew that while she had an excellent reputation within the industry, her appearance was vitally important when it came to making an impact in her new role.

I would class myself as petite and I love wearing high heels because they give me confidence and make me feel fantastic. A few years ago I had to wear flat shoes for six months after injuring my ankle. People (mostly men) made comments about why I wasn't wearing heels and that I looked better wearing heels. The comment about "looking better" was inappropriate but it did bring home the fact of how much people notice one's appearance. Once, when my nails weren't done, they picked up on that too. High heels and painted nails are part of my personal image so that is what they associate me with and they are surprised if they see something different. Other small things that can make a big difference are things like making sure your shoes are polished. I was left wondering after these incidents if the women noticed my appearance in such detail but were just too polite to say.

Dressing up or dressing down?

When I am going to a client meeting, I wear my business clothes no matter who I am going to see. Whether I am going into a design agency where they all wear jeans or a financial services provider where they wear suits, they are all expecting to see a lawyer so I make sure that I look like one.

Between my 20s and mid 30s, I predominantly wore suits. I am now at an age when I feel I can wear a jacket and a dress which gives me more variety but I still want to look like the lawyer I am. You need to work out your own dress code; it's part of your personal brand. If you're creative, such as a designer or copywriter then you have more flexibility in your approach. I recall attending a networking group where the electrician would turn up in his work clothes which was great! I never forgot that he was an electrician and what company he worked for. The outfit was appropriate for those early breakfast meetings!

However, the issue I have about dressing down whether as a dress code or even just for dress-down days, is how it affects your thinking. If you are wearing jeans and a t-shirt, then a message is sent to your brain that you're more relaxed. If you wear a suit, your posture and even your thinking is different. This applies to a lady wearing high heels too. There was an interesting piece of research done by Brigham Young University[28] which showed that if a woman was wearing very high heels when shopping, she tended to make a more balanced decision because standing in heels focused her mind. If you're in flats you can hang around forever and you tend to be a bit more random about your choices.

I know a lady who runs a well-known tea shop attached to a farm and she likes to attend networking events. If she walked in wearing wellies she would get judged a certain way. Interestingly when I attended an event with a young colleague from my firm, she commented afterwards that she

---

[28] 25 August 2013 News Release 'Wearing high heels can change the way you shop', Brigham Young University.

had expected to see this woman, who was immaculate in every way, to be wearing wellies! It just goes to show that we all have preconceptions of what we expect people to be like. Sometimes we have to adhere to them, whereas at other times we have to intentionally move away from them. A lot of public figures often change their appearance to be perceived in a different light.

What you wear is important, not only to how others perceive you but also to how you perceive yourself and how you behave. It affects how you talk and how you come across when you're speaking. How you speak is influenced by what you're wearing because you're conscious of where you are and of your image.

Of course, you learn to adapt according to the circumstances. A client invited me to an annual event held at a pub. It's a casual event and I don't do casual – casual to me is what I am at home. So I still dress smartly and for the first few years that I attended this event, I wore a smart dress, which you are allowed to do if you're coming from the office. Last year I wore jeans with a jacket and blouse from the office and I had heels on so I was still in work mode. I was semi-relaxed because I knew the other attendees by now. We had already established a relationship and had moved on to the stage of reconfirming it so I wasn't introducing myself as somebody new. It is important to wear what you think represents you and how you want to be perceived in the industry.

Sometimes, of course, an opportunity to network comes along when you are least expecting it. When I did a 10K run a few years ago, I met a lovely woman who has since become a good friend, while wearing jogging bottoms and a t-shirt! And there were certainly no heels! Normally that would have made me feel shy and introverted - because I wasn't in the right gear for networking, but we were both chatty and open-minded and it was fine.

Personal image and what it says about you is important, but so is your personality. Don't be afraid to show people who you are, what your interests are, and demonstrate your expertise.

Chapter 4

Preparing to network

"Being your best is not so much about overcoming the barriers other people place in front of you as it is about overcoming the barriers we place in front of ourselves." Kieren Perkins[29]

"Success is where preparation and opportunity meet." Bobby Unser[30]

To succeed at networking, you should not simply just turn up at an event. You will always feel slightly on the back foot if you do. Preparation is the key. Think about what you want to achieve from networking, make sure you have all the tools (e.g. your personal brand, your business cards etc) ready

---

[29] An Australian former competition swimmer, four-time Olympic medallist, and former world record-holder in three events.

[30] Retired American automobile racer.

and develop your 'elevator pitch'[31].

Formal events

First of all, you need know the reason/objective for you to attend an event. For instance, I recently debated whether to attend a black tie event that involved most of the alternative finance lending industry. I decided the time and cost was worth it to meet most of the industry in one room. My objective was to promote Legatus Law's services and touch base with connections I had already made with the aim of getting a follow up meeting. As a result, I ended up with two profitable meetings.

The point is to know why you are attending the event in the first place. It is your time and your personal and company's brand. For example, I am often invited to attend events that can last up to six or seven hours. I need to decide whether it's worth spending all that time. Always remember, particularly if a company is sending you to an event, it is your personal brand/you as a person that people are 'buying'.

A variety of factors will influence my decision about whether to attend:

1. My host has kindly invited me so it's important to attend to continue to grow and build that relationship (but if time or circumstances do not permit you to

---

[31] Defined later in this chapter.

attend, then apologise for declining but try to provide an explanation as opposed to just a "sorry cannot make it" - after all, they made the effort to invite you!).

2. You already have an objective in place. So for instance when I attend the ICAEW (The Institute of Chartered Accountants in England and Wales) Dinner or Construction Lunch, or Manufacturers Dinner, this gives me the opportunity to meet new people. When I attend YABL (Yorkshire Asset Based Lenders), Dealmakers, Institute of Directors events or the Races (horses), the objective is to see people that I already know, getting 5-10 minutes with someone at an event is easier than trying to organise a coffee, particularly if they have a busy diary. I'll inevitably be introduced to new contacts there as well.

Choose the event carefully. If you are just starting out in the industry or have a fairly new and growing business, you want to create strong links in the local community. It may be that you just want to meet other people in your industry and build connections. Whatever the motive, you must have a reason to justify any time, energy and money you spend at the event.

I've always been a big believer in measuring and quantifying my time. I suppose that stems from being a lawyer! So when it comes to networking, I record what events I've attended, who I've met and whether those contacts have led to an introduction, a referral, or an opportunity. That way I can see the value that's come from each event and each contact made. You will be surprised to see how much can come from networking.

There are some things when you attend an event that you must must must have! Your stock 'must haves' include:

- Business cards
- The right attire
- Your personal brand
- Your character/armour
- Knowing your message
- Knowing your objective.

Before the event

If you are attending a formal event, try to obtain a list of attendees beforehand. This will enable you to consider who you want to meet and also gives you time to carry out some research on the attendees. If you are attending a meeting, or even just having a coffee with someone, it is again important to know as much as possible about the person you are meeting to maximise your time during the meeting. If you are attending events try to highlight the attendees you want to meet on the list provided. For example, the TMA

UK[32] London events always provide a delegate list beforehand. So before I attend each event, I study the list to firstly see if there are any new attendees and secondly to see who is on the list I know so I can ensure I say "hello" to them, in order to continue the relationship that I have built.

Ensure that you have ample business cards with you, even for the events where you believe you will know most of the people there. You never know what might happen! I have met too many people who have forgotten to take their business cards with them, or said "I didn't think I needed them today!" The real problem arises when you and the other party have both forgotten your business cards! Your business card acts as a reminder the next day to the person you have given your card to. It is another way of making your presence known and hopefully will lead to a follow up. We have already talked about your personal brand and image in chapter 3.

Before the event you will need to know what your elevator pitch is. This is your message. The term 'elevator pitch' is widely credited to Ilene Rosenzweig and Michael Caruso (while he was editor for Vanity Fair) for its origin[33]. The theory is that you are able to describe and sell your service or product in the time it takes the elevator/lift to go from

---

[32] The Turnaround Management Association (TMA) was founded in the USA in 1988, and is a non-profit organisation for practitioners in corporate renewal and turnaround management.

[33] Wikipedia 2015

one floor to the next, leaving you between 30-60 seconds to get your message across. This is a very useful tool, as it helps you understand what your message is and helps you to hone that message into something that's simple and succinct. For example, mine is "Hi I'm Rashmi Dubé, fabulous lawyer with Legatus Law. I help protect you and your business with all its legal needs." People tend to focus on 'fabulous' – because this is not often used alongside the word 'lawyer' – the two seem incompatible. It gets the listener's attention, at least for the next 30 seconds after which I will ask them, if I have not already done so, what they do. The elevator pitch is a useful tool also in the everyday world. When a neighbour asks what you do for a living they don't want to hear you say "well I am lawyer who drafts contracts, agreements, distribution agreements, manager buy-out's and buy-in's, disputes over shareholders or partnership agreements, litigation, dealing with all forms of disputes including construction and engineering disputes"! This is too long and complicated and frankly you have lost them.

"I am a fabulous lawyer" - I say this because most lawyers say, "I am a lawyer for my sins" or something in that vein which is negative and probably turns people off. I had a friend once say, as she also pointed to me, that she was a "penny to the pound lawyer." I corrected her immediately saying she might be but I was definitely not! By starting off with "fabulous lawyer," the other person is hearing a word that they do not tend to hear in an introduction or description and is rarely associated with lawyers. They will therefore remember that I am a lawyer. The second part of the elevator pitch/speech is what I or Legatus Law do which is "protect you and your business" so the person understands that we are business lawyers. This naturally leads to questions and a more in-depth discussion. So people will ask if I cover employment law or tell me they are buying a business or need a contract drafting and enquire if that is something I could look into. I am not saying my elevator pitch is perfect – I believe it can be improved and is constantly being redefined and tweaked. I suspect by the time this book is published it would have changed again.

Some tips for preparing your elevator pitch

In essence, the elevator pitch is a brief and persuasive 30-60 second speech that you will use to generate a discussion.

1. Identify your goal. Mine is to talk about Legatus Law in general terms but also to ensure that I have conveyed that I am a lawyer and the managing director of the firm.

2. Explain what you do. This is hard because you need to be succinct and have the ability to say what you or your organisation does, e.g. we are lawyers who help and protect businesses.

3. If possible, communicate a USP (unique selling point). What makes you/your business or employer stand out from the crowd? For instance, mine is as a business owner - having started the business I offer legal advice but have empathy for the commercial requirements of a business and therefore bring a commercial awareness to the advice I provide.

4. Practise – by yourself, on colleagues, with friends or family. The more you practise the more you will become comfortable with the words/terms and style of delivery. And remember - it is ok to smile when speaking to people!

Business cards

Always always always take some business cards with you wherever you go. You just don't know who you may meet where - such as the start line of a 10K run![34] The most common mistake people make is to forget their business cards when they change outfits to go out. This happened to me a few years back at the Childline Annual Charity dinner at the Landmark Hotel in London. I was rushing and hastily changed my outfit and, as any respectable lady would do at a black tie event, changed my handbag for an evening bag. Yes, you've got it - I forgot to put my business cards in the

---

[34] The full story appears later on in this chapter.

bag. Even on holiday I take a few – I recently met a couple at the airport looking to sell their business – clearly they needed a lawyer!

The next question really is how you carry your business cards. My business cards are white and the logo is red and gold. So I have to be careful not to discolour the cards but also I don't want the cards to be damaged. This is your shop window for your organisation and more importantly for you. You are telling the other person how much you care about your presentation. I have a card holder which holds a few cards and then the rest remain in the box that they originally came in. Most people like the business card holder and comment on that. Again I have done something that has made me memorable in people's minds.

How to hand over and receive a business card

This can, of course, vary culturally so be aware. In general terms for the UK I am often surprised at the number of people who simply start talking at me and then hand me their business card. They have neither engaged with me and at no point did I ask them to give me their business card. Here are RR Rashmi's Rules of business cards:

1. Engage with the person first, then ask them for their card.

2. Do not give your card out unless the other person requests it. You can ask them in some instances if it is ok to give them your card.

I once took some students networking and gave them a target of five business cards that night. I knew one of the students wanted to get to know lawyers as she was looking for a training contract. I introduced to her to a firm and left her to have a chat with two lawyers from that firm. Later I noted that she had only acquired one business card and when I asked her why she had not got the other lawyer's card she replied, "they worked for the same firm so I didn't see the need". I explained that networking was all about the individuals as well as the organisations and that it was important to build one-to-one relationships and so it would have been good to get the other person's card as well.

As it happens, both lawyers went on to start their own firm. If the students had taken both cards and the time to build those relationships they might have had a great opportunity to ask for paralegal experience. Remember, networking isn't about collecting business cards, it's about getting to know people and keeping in touch.

Another point on preparation – do you know where you will keep the business cards you collect? Sometimes it is easier if you have jacket pockets.

Informal networking

This can be anywhere, anytime. So always be prepared. Be armed with your message/elevator pitch and always have some business cards with you. You never know who you might meet. Being prepared, for me, means having red lipstick, business cards and my personal brand in terms of my attire.

You have to be open-minded when it comes to meeting new people and understand that you can meet people who could be important to your business or your personal life in ways you can never imagine. Equally that you can be just as important to them. The worst thing to do is be dismissive of anyone you meet.

I did my first 10K run back in July 2009 and I met up with a dear friend, Jill, one of the girls from my book club who was also running. We had arranged to meet at the start line. She introduced me to Tracy, a friend of hers who she was running with. They told me they were aiming to do the race in under an hour whereas I was happy to achieve under 1hr 30! We had a bit of banter; they liked the sign I had attached to my back saying "Rashmi Dubé - slow moving traffic". Then the two of them set off like gazelles. Luckily I had arranged to meet them at the pub after the race! When I turned up at the pub sometime later, Tracy was still there so I had a good chat with her. This is informal networking: we talked about what we did, exchanged business cards and arranged to meet up for a coffee. Next thing I knew, Tracy and I became great friends and ended up networking together at the same events. I see this as informal networking.

Chapter 5

The networking event

"*Every time you dive, you hope you'll see something new - some new species. Sometimes the ocean gives you a gift, sometimes it doesn't.*"
James Cameron[35]

You've arrived at the event! Trepidation will knock on your door, but you're prepared. You may not be ready to make a big splash but dip your toe in and you'll soon be swimming along nicely.

Formal networking - arriving at the event

If it's a formal event, you will be asked to register. While you're registering, you can ask the organiser to introduce

---

[35] A Canadian filmmaker, inventor, engineer, philanthropist, and deep-sea explorer.

you to people from the attendees list if you have had one in advance. So, for example, if there's someone in particular you want to meet, you can see if they have arrived. If the registration desk cannot help, and you do not know anyone in the room ask them if they can introduce you to someone in the specific sector you're interested in, e.g. "are there any accountants here today?" This is often a good way to get the ball rolling. Walking into a room not knowing anyone can be daunting so getting someone to make the first introduction makes it a lot easier.

Alternatively, make your way to the refreshment stand, there's bound to be other people there you can start talking to, perhaps by saying, "have you been to these events before?" "What are they like?" "I am looking forward to the speaker today. Do you think they will cover such and such in their talk?" Just take care not to get stuck there! Sometimes people seem to handcuff themselves to the refreshments area, too nervous to move away, but it's a false safe zone. These people aren't benefitting themselves or their company - in fact they could be damaging their brand by not engaging more. It might be better for them to go back to the office and send someone else. Just remember you are spending time and money being at the event. Make the most of it.

Once you have got yourself a drink, take a look around the room and try to spot people who are standing by themselves. Approaching people who are on their own is a good way to start. Remember they would probably love for someone to come up to them and talk to them; it could be that they are feeling shy and nervous. They might be looking at their phones – this is bad – never use your phone as a prop like this because it makes it harder for people to come and talk to you. Having spotted someone, this is where you can employ your false confidence (see chapter 2). Drawing on my character's ability to engage with people, I would go over and say: "Hi, how are you? I'm Rashmi, so nice to meet you. And you are?" Ask them to tell you all about themselves – always let them speak. People are comfortable with telling you who they are and it makes them less nervous. This also gives you time to settle in. Be sure to listen! Pay attention to what they are saying and be present in the conversation. Spend a bit of time talking about yourself, when appropriate. Remember the other person may be shy and forget to ask about you. Don't stay in the conversation too long.[36] See if they know anyone they can introduce you to, otherwise move on, politely.

Make your presence known

At large, formal events, I always carry a golf pencil with me in my handbag and I write on one of my business cards the number of the tables I want to visit. This might be the tables where there are people I know or those where there are people I would like to introduce myself to. So, in between courses I stand up, having asked the people at my table that

---

[36] There is no hard and fast rule to this. Judge each situation on its own merits. Trust your judgment.

I have already spoken to, to excuse me, and go over to one of those tables and say hi, even if it's just for two minutes, after which I return to my own table. This is a good tactic for getting to see as many people as possible, especially if there are 20 or 30 tables with 3,000 people there. It's important to circulate to prevent missing those people. It isn't helpful to say, after the event, "I wish I'd seen that person and managed to get my face in front of them." I would say, "Do it then! Don't wish it, just do it!" I love that Nike slogan – just do it!

Say you're at table 2 and you want to go to table 42. Dinner has just finished and dessert is on its way. Just get up, walk over to table 42, and find the person there that you wanted to say hello to. If they're in conversation, simply say: "Sorry to interrupt, I just wanted to say hi, I hope you're well." Nine times out of ten they'll be happy to see you and introduce you to the person they're talking to.

The hardest part is getting up out of your chair in the first place and walking over. Just ask yourself, what's the worst that could happen? The person you wanted to speak to is not at the table? That's fine! You've got a backup table, you've written a list! If they are not at the table, even better – you can go to the table and say, "Excuse me, I thought Tom Jones was at this table?" If they confirm that he is in attendance then I simply say, "can you let him know Rashmi stopped by to say hello?" The message may or may not get to him but at least you have tried. If possible ask the person's name when you are leaving the message. This has the added advantage that you have also introduced yourself to them. This is what I call my 'sniper approach' to networking!

It is, of course, equally important to find time for longer conversations. I tend to leave that till later on in the event.

How to get networking right – a scenario

If you arrive at an organised networking drinks event there may well be between 100 and 200 people there. In these circumstances, the best thing to do is find someone you know. Go up to them, greet them and find out how they are and what's new with them. Tell them what's new with you - this acts as a good way of letting both parties know if there are any changes and new developments in the services being offered. If you look around and you can't see anyone else that you know (or at least anyone you know you want to talk to – just because you know someone doesn't mean you want to talk to them!) then ask the person you're speaking to if there's anyone that they could introduce you to. It is always better to be specific here if possible. If there is a particular person or sector that you want to go for, then even better. Be as sniper in your approach as possible.

When the introduction has been made and you're chatting to the new person, remember the rule that you have: two ears

and

 one mouth

So use them in proportion. Listen to what they're saying, let them talk about themselves, ask them questions. Be present and listen attentively. Don't be afraid to just have a conversation with someone. Wait for them to ask you what you do then give them your elevator pitch (see chapter 4). Ask general questions to find out what they're like. Try commenting on local events, sport etc to see if they like sports or theatre, films or art. If there's a national event going on then ask them what they think about that. It's all about getting to know that person. Then ask them for their business card. Be sure to place the card in a safe place for the follow up (see chapter 6).

Then ask them if they can introduce you to someone else. Remember, a warm introduction is better than you simply approaching somebody. The best way to do this is ask them if they know anyone in the room or have met anyone today. If they say yes, ask them if they are happy to introduce you to that person. In some instances you may also be able to introduce the person you are speaking to, to another person at the event. I prefer to help others in this way, it is just a nicer way of networking. Don't forget to thank them for the introduction and tell them that you appreciate it. They will feel delighted that they've been able to help and the new person you've been introduced to will also feel good because they might be able to see potential in speaking to you. Additionally, you'll feel pleased because you've been introduced to somebody new. Equally if you can introduce the person to someone you have spoken to the same goodwill applies. Networking is hard so one of my rules is help introduce people to one another at an event.

Then you start again with the new contact, by asking them questions and finding out about what they do. For example, if you meet someone from a construction company or department you can ask them what they specifically specialise in, e.g. are they a quantity surveyor or involved in engineering projects or act as expert witnesses in a particular field? It might be something totally different to what you imagine. I attended a pre-Christmas event once, through an invitation from friends who were part of the construction world. They asked me if I could introduce them to people from different specialties. I came across a chemical engineer who had recently passed her exams as a mediator. This sparked a discussion, which led to another meeting with a colleague, which in turn allowed Legatus Law to do a presentation on "The role of experts in mediation".

Networking on your own can be hard, and sometimes it is easier to attend an event with people you know. This allows you to refer back to them and ask who they have met and exchange notes, as it were. However, far too often, groups or pairs of people from the same company will attend an event and only speak to the people they've come with, and they don't capitalise on the opportunity to speak to others. I noted this recently at a conference. After the dinner people from one global company sat with their own group and did not socialise or network with others. On a more day to day basis this occurs when two or more individuals are sent from a company to an event, they stick together simply because it is easier and safer for them. Again this is a waste of time and money. The purpose of having more than one of you at the same event is to be able to work the room more efficiently. If you want to network or bond with your fellow colleagues – arrange or organise a specific event for that purpose.

Hit by another swimmer

Although most attendees go to networking events with a positive attitude and with a genuine desire to meet and socialise with people, occasionally you can run into difficulties.

People are insecure and scared of being at an event and can sometimes inadvertently come across as rude or difficult. I tend to find humour often defuses the situation. In most instances the other party are not even aware what they have done or said. The important thing is not to take offence and not to take any criticism personally, which can be hard to do if you are already nervous about being at the event.

Identifying groups

It is useful to understand the different groups of people that you might find at a networking event.

A closed group – where people stand in a group with their backs to you. The group, often a circle or with very closed

body language, is not inviting anyone in to join their conversation. This happens either because an intense conversation is taking place and they want to finish it without interruption; or because they want to stay talking to their friends or even to their own colleagues from the office, as they feel uncomfortable being at the event and speaking to other people. it is best to avoid groups that demonstrate this body language, There is no point breaking into this group. You will recognise this group with practise.

People standing alone. These people are often shy and not sure how to approach people in conversation. This is ideal time for you to use your false confidence. Approach them and initiate a conversation.

Open groups – two or three people talking together whose body language is telling you that it's fine to come and join their group. They might even be asking for help because they don't know how to get away from the people they're talking to!

Exiting

I have discussed above that a good way to exit a conversation is to ask if you could be introduced to someone the other person knows or has met, but this may not always work. Therefore you need to be able to extract yourself from the conversation, otherwise you may find that the person with whom you been talking is so nervous they don't want to let you go because you have become their safe zone. There are a number of ways of doing this:

1. See if you can find an 'open' group of people and say to the other person, "let's go and have a chat with those people."

2. If you are unable to do that, you can go and refresh

your drink or simply say, "excuse me I think I will go and mingle – we are here after all to network." Most people will not mind.

When networking I find certain things work well for me. I call it my networking étiquette. It may not work for you, but I thought I would mention it. As I have said, I have a business card holder when I am networking, but I do not just hand my business cards out. I often find it rude when people just hand their cards out without being asked. I will hand over my card if a suggestion has been made within the group that business cards should be exchanged. In a one-to-one scenario, once you have exchanged business cards I find it polite to take some time to look at the person's business card. In the UK we have a bad habit of being given a card, barely looking at it and then just placing into our handbag or pocket. Instead, take the time to see who has handed their card to you and what it looks and feels like. A lot can be gleaned from a business card. The paper and print quality tell me how much value someone places on their brand, for instance. Networking étiquette varies country to country and it is advisable to equate yourself with the étiquette of the country you're operating in.

Networking skills

It is important to remember when networking to:

1. Listen – two ears, one mouth – be present in the conversation and really listen.

2. Ask open questions to enable the other person to speak. An open question is the opposite of a closed question which is one that can be answered with a simple yes or a no. Open questions tend to start with what, where, when, how and why.

3. Avoid being pushy – don't sell.

4. Get to know people and decide on the relationships you want to build. Take your time to get to know the person, don't bombard them with who you are, what you do and what you want. Remember the focus is on building relationships and not looking for transactions.

These skills apply whether you are networking with people you have just met or people you already know.

Alcohol

Yes alcohol is often available at these events. Many people use alcohol to be sociable and as part of their networking regime. Remember, that most organisations would expect their employees to represent the company in a responsible manner. There's often a learning curve to getting the balance right. I leave it you to decide whether or not to partake. All I will say is that the Drinkaware charity[37] advises sensible drinking.

---

[37] *Drinkaware* is an independent charity working to reduce alcohol misuse and harm in the UK.

Informal networking

Informal networking can take place anywhere, Like the start of a 10K run (see chapter 4). However, in most instances, informal networking happens at organised events such as the horse races, an informal lunch or annual get together at a pub. All these events may be 'organised' but they are less formal than a black tie event. The environment is a lot more relaxed and anything can happen. But the same skills apply. Someone who once worked at my practice, who was new to networking, was going to a fashion ball. I reminded her to take her business cards. She said, "I thought you said it was a social event so I wasn't networking." We all do it – think that we are simply socialising and not networking! One Christmas we went out as a firm to celebrate and everyone, myself included, forgot to take their business cards – needless to say we met someone whose company required assistance with a dispute. Although we swapped details, it did not make for a good impression.

We should have remembered that you are constantly networking. Networking is all about building and maintaining valued relationships. When you build up your business contacts, it might not feel like something you do for love! But you will be spending time with them and it's important you like the people you do business with. They may even become very close friends and developing successful relationships will lead to your and the other person's success. Care about the relationships you are forming.

An example of building long term relationships happened as a result of chance. I attended the York Races with a group of ladies and four of us got left behind – yes the coach just left us! How rude! Luckily one of the ladies knew someone who was a guest of a company of asset valuers. They kindly gave us a ride back to Leeds, which led to some very good friendships developing over the years. It also led to an introduction to another branch within their company.

Some of the most informal networking I do is on the train. I often commute on the train between London and Leeds and I love the train ride because I never know who I might meet and where it may all end up! It can often be quite random. I got speaking to one lady on the train, which led me to the co-editor of this book! That is networking at its best.

Internal networking

One of the most important places for informal networking is in your office, with your work colleagues and managers. This is important at any point of your career. Regardless of your sector the same principles apply. It is very important to build good relationships with those you work with.

Networking with your fellow colleagues is important – going for meals and drinks etc. but it is also important that you understand the wider circle your company operates in. By joining organisations/clubs/groups within the organisation you will get a better understanding of who people are in the business and they get a better understanding of who you are. As always in networking, it's about building relationships and raising your profile within the company. Many, many years ago (the 1990's) I was working as a paralegal at a law firm. At a social event, the heads of the department and the partner were socialising with us. I spent my time first getting to know my other colleagues then talking with the heads and chatting with the partner. This led to the development of long term relationships with the people I was working with.

Things to remember/be guided by:

1. Don't be a taker – bring something to the table. My philosophy on networking and general way I approach many things in life is help others along the way. This particularly applies as you become a more established networker – see who you can either offer assistance to and also bring something to the table for those you are trying to connect with. This is how you develop a long term relationship. If you simply 'take' the relationship will be short-lived. The objective is always to build long term valued relationships.

2. Don't demand access to other people's network. People have spent time cultivating and nurturing their network - why should they simply allow you to have access to it? Earn the introduction.

3. Remember, it is all about the relationship - you don't need to sell. People want to get to know you first. They will understand what you do if your message is clear.

Chapter 6

The follow up

"*You ain't supposed to get salmon when they're swimming upstream to spawn. But if you're hungry, you do.*" Loretta Lynn[38]

"*One reason so few of us achieve what we truly want is that we never direct our focus; we never concentrate our power. Most people dabble their way through life, never deciding to master anything in particular.*" Tony Robbins[39]

"*It's all to do with the training: you can do a lot if you're properly trained.*" HRH Queen Elizabeth II

---

[38] American country music singer-songwriter whose work spans nearly 60 years.

[39] American motivational speaker, personal finance instructor, and self-help author.

The follow up is the hurdle we all fall at, myself included. This is what I would call my Achilles heel. Yet, like the quotes above suggest, if we can focus and train ourselves, create the right habits, the follow up should be easy and become second nature. As I read these words, it sounds simple, but in practise, it can be the hardest thing to do especially if you are a small medium enterprise and are busy with the day job which is in fact five different roles wrapped up into one. Where is the time?! But it is all down to you!!

A friend once had a meeting with a large accountancy firm in London who asked for more information about what his company did, in terms of construction and engineering. He promised to send an email providing this information. Once he got back to the office though, he became engrossed in the daily grind. And forgot to do the follow up! Yes, an opportunity lost! But it's a common mistake made by all.

We spend time, money and energy going to events and meeting people but then we fail to follow up within good time or at all. We find ourselves saying that we meet all these people but this never seems to generate any business opportunities. That is because we are not creating our own 'opportunities'. Throughout this book I have explained that networking is all about building relationships that are long term, as people will do business with people they like and networking affords you the opportunity to support others in their quests. But in order to build those long term relationships you have to put the work in, long term.

Opportunity gained!

I gave a talk at a university on networking and the importance for postgraduates who were still studying of getting out there and attempting to network. After the talk I stayed behind to see who would come up and speak to me – in other words take the opportunity to follow up with me. I also gave them the option to contact me via email. Some students connected with me on LinkedIn and two of them contacted me to see if I could give them practical experience of networking. Fantastic! I took them to an event called the Yorkshire Mafia. It was scary for them but they dived into the deep end and started swimming using the tools I had given them to help navigate their evening. The follow up can take many forms – you just have to do it! It will help to ensure you build that relationship whether it turns into friendship or business.

What are the basics of the follow up?

So you have attended the event: you feel elated - you've met lots of great people and you've collected a whole load of business cards. Well done! But there is still a lot of ground to cover. All you have done is dip your toe into the world of networking and made initial contact with people. So what next? So often we think, "I am busy, I must get some work done. I was out of the office so must catch up on all those emails! I will email or contact those people later." Then a week, a month, two months go by and you end up with a collection of what I call 'fish' business cards. Because after they've sat on your desk for a while they begin to smell! The follow up is about keeping the business cards fresh, the contacts fresh.

Here are my tips for the follow up. Although they work for me, that is not to say this is the right procedure for you, but in the early days of networking every piece of advice helps until you develop your own strategy.

The first thing to do, immediately after having attended an event or met a new person, is make a note on their business card of the day's date. Include any facts or insights you may know about the person. This might feel a bit time-consuming but it is worth it in the long run. It means that when you meet or speak to them again you'll know when and where you met them first and be reminded of something about them that might help you in your conversation. There are smartphone apps available which enable you to save the business card details onto the phone and you can add notes too. But if you do as much networking as I do then you may not want to have every person's name in your phone.

LinkedIn is my next step. I will see if my new contacts are on LinkedIn and if so I will connect with them and remind them where we met. If you haven't already done so, get a LinkedIn profile. In my view, LinkedIn is a must in business. It is not like Facebook or Twitter. It is an excellent way to display your expertise/CV for the business community to see. It means you're in contact with your connections every time you make a post. It is an excellent forum for showcasing your experience and expertise and a good way to keep your contacts in one place. Please give consideration though to your employer's social media policy. If you are an employer make sure you have a policy in place[40]. When you are linking with someone don't just send them the standard message set up by LinkedIn, say something personal. This person has probably made some impression on you so let them know. This also helps because people can get spammed with invitations from unknowns, and if you have left it for a week or so it acts as a good reminder of who you are. In addition your LinkedIn profile is a good way to showcase your talents, attributes and what you do. If people are not on LinkedIn, send them an email to say how lovely it was to meet them.

If I think it is appropriate, I will arrange to meet people for a coffee.

I also have a client relationship management (CRM) system[41] in place. Whenever anyone within the firm has been to an event and meets someone they will enter that person's details onto the CRM database. This helps us monitor what's happening with that person in terms of follow

---

[40] As an employer you may want to incorporate the use of LinkedIn into the contract of employment.

[41] A database to monitor networking events and who we have met as a firm.

up. A simple Excel spreadsheet can be used to record this information, if you'd prefer. I find this system useful when it comes to measuring how much time we have spent at networking events and what the outcome has been. This makes it easy to evaluate the value of different events.

Meeting for coffee

To make the most of your coffee meeting I recommend a number of things:

1. Prepare for the meeting beforehand. This may be a one-to-one meeting but it's still networking and is likely to explore a variety of avenues. The better prepared you are the more you'll get out of the meeting. Research the person to see what you can bring to the table

2. Ensure you know what you want from the meeting. In most cases it is to strengthen the relationship you are trying to cultivate. Spend time getting to know the other person and their business, what they are looking for and whether it is possible for you to help them in some way.

3. Remember some meetings are just to get to know the person. Time is always a factor so choose your meetings well.

The follow up is time well spent. It is, in fact, the aspect of networking you really must carry out. But it is often the part of the networking that we are not very good at. And yet it benefits us the most. It is critical both in terms of the opportunities that can arise and in making sure you use your time productively. You should spend just as much time in the follow up as you do preparing for and attending the event itself.

Bringing something to the table

An insolvency practice, based in London and Manchester, decided to open a branch in Leeds. It had taken a table at a charity event in Leeds. I went up to the table, introduced myself and asked them what they were looking for in terms of building relationships in Leeds. Then, over the next few months, I made introductions where I could. The idea was to develop a good working relationship, which we now have.

Other times you may have a follow up meeting with new people you have met, simply because they are just lovely people. This has happened to me many times. I once arranged to meet for coffee, with no ulterior motives, and as a result made two very good friends. We have never done any business, but I am grateful to have them in my life as dear friends.

There is, I'm afraid, no magic wand that will make business opportunities just happen. You have to put in the work and you have to follow up! It is like with your friends, if neither of you arranges to meet up, then it never happens!

Chapter 7

A little more networking – is it social?

"Social media is an amazing tool, but it's really the face-to-face interaction that makes a long-term impact." Felicia Day[42]

"We don't have a choice on whether we DO social media, the questions is how well we DO it." Erik Qualman[43]

Throughout my life, what I have found is that 'networking' can happen any time, any place. Take my mother, for example: I was just finishing my A 'levels and was looking for a summer job to save money for university. My mother

---

[42] An American actress, comedian, and writer.

[43] An American author of *Socialnomics*, which according to WorldCat, is held in 1090 libraries. He is also the author of *Digital Leader* and *What Happens in Vegas Stays on YouTube*.

started chatting to a lady at the bus stop, who happened to be running the DVLA in Reading and she agreed to look at my CV. I got a job from that as they needed temporary staff to cover an influx of paperwork and holiday leave. That, folks, is networking or "being social" as my mum would say.

A more recent example was when I working in London and decided to stay in central London. I had finished work late and went to order some bar food. The bar was busy so I asked to share a table with a young lady. As it transpired she was from the USA and was in town visiting and looking for legal advice! I only found this out because I chose to engage in conversation with her. It would have been easy for us to both get lost in our mobile phones. Or even worse I could have ordered room service and then we would never have met!

Personal contacts can also act as a form of informal networking. My book club ladies are a great source of inspiration and loving friends whom I adore! They have always been there to support me at every juncture, as I them. So when I told them how hard it was to find someone to assist part-time in the business I was running then - Liquid Recovery, a debt recovery and credit control company - they came to the rescue, suggesting an ex-student from the Law School.

Sometimes situations make you change the way you network or the arena in which you network. I once spent a lot of my time travelling from Leeds, West Yorkshire, to see my family and friends in London. As I was also spending a great deal of money on train fares I decided that perhaps a more efficient use of my time and money would be achieved by staying in London and developing contacts there. I decided to review my LinkedIn contacts in order to ascertain who was connected to who and to see if I could get an appointment to meet with them. Surprisingly a lot of people responded to my call once I explained that I obtained their contact details via LinkedIn and that we were connected through a mutual contact. Through the meetings that took place I managed to build my London practice which led to Legatus Law opening an office in London a year ahead of schedule.

This demonstrates how useful social media can be when it comes to networking[44]. Social media gives us a way to build our contacts and enables us to put ourselves in front of people to allow them to see our expertise. What I have found is that Twitter and LinkedIn are very useful tools for Legatus Law as they provide us with the ability to showcase our individual expertise as business lawyers and mediators. They also present us with opportunities which allow us to promote the firm as a whole, as a niche corporate/ commercial/disputes and construction and engineering firm.

As I have always said in this book, this is my perspective on

---

[44] An article written for London Economics on my view of social media and its impact can be found at page 134.

matters. I am not an expert in social media and if you want to learn more you will need to contact a specialist in this area. What I can talk about is my experience and how I view things.

We touched upon LinkedIn earlier in the previous chapter. LinkedIn is an excellent tool to connect with people, create a database of contacts, to showcase both your expertise and that of the company if you are also a business owner. Once you have created a profile, try and get people to endorse you or to provide testimonials. This adds credibility to your expertise and CV. LinkedIn is also an excellent platform for expressing your views by joining and contributing to group discussions. You can also post your blogs, articles or general information that you think may be of use to others on LinkedIn. Note that I have said, "of use to others." Do not sell. It is a turn off and the idea is really to help others with the information you provide.

There are other platforms besides LinkedIn and perhaps this is where you should bring in specialists that can advise you on what would work best for you or your company, in terms of its message and brand when it comes to social media. You have Twitter, YouTube and Facebook (and other platforms)– which can all work wonders. Twitter and Instagram can showcase a variety of messages.

My main principle for social media is to keep business

related[45] activity and personal activity separate. I have my own personal accounts with Facebook and Twitter which remain quite separate from the business accounts. My own thoughts should not be related to that of the business.

Social media is here and it is staying. It is growing and it is how a lot of people are communicating. For some of us it can feel like a brave new world but let's embrace it and make it work for us.

For me though, there is no substitute for the face to face meeting. I would say this is particularly true of long distance business relationships with clients/customers and suppliers. Get on the plane and meet them if you can, don't hide behind emails or video conferences or Skype. At some point that face to face bond will help your relationship with them later down the line. However, do not underestimate the use of social media and get the experts to provide you with the right advice. It can prove to be invaluable to your business and/or career.

---

[45] I have a separate Twitter account for the business and my private life. The business Twitter account is for information that will be of use or interest to the general public and the personal Twitter account is for my meandering thoughts.

Chapter 8

Does gender make a difference?

"It's all about people. It's about networking and being nice to people and not burning any bridges. [...] in the end it is people that are going to hire you." Mike Davidson[46]

"I don't see myself in terms of gender or sex, simply as Rashmi." Rashmi Dubé

Gender - does it make a difference to networking? Men and women - are we the same? Do we have to be? Why do men and women have single-sex networking groups?

These are some of the questions that I have thought about when writing this book. More and more I have come across

---

[46] Quoted in *Building Bridges: Collaboration Within and Beyond the Academic Library* by Anne Langley, Edward Gray, K T L Vaughan.

single-sex networking events. Why? Which then led me to think, do men and women network differently generally and does it change even more when we mix? If that is the case – how does that affect our 'internal' networking within our company with our work colleagues? These are questions that deserve a whole book to themselves. But they do have a part to play in this book as I believe gender differences can have an impact on how we behave when we network. So it would be wrong for me to ignore the topic completely.

As times have changed it is becoming a requirement to be able to do business development alongside your day job. The question has arisen: do men and women approach networking differently? Is there a difference in approach based upon gender? Over time there has been a lot of research into how men and women communicate that indicates that men and women think differently and therefore inherently approach things differently, for example, their negotiation styles[47]. My theory (it could be because I am a woman) is that women approach networking in a less 'transactional' manner. That is to say when having a conversation I believe men are focused on a specific target whilst women approach conversations in a more holistic way. Although having said that, men appear, to me, to be very good at building long term relationships. But once they have

---

[47] "Gender differences in leadership styles and the impact within corporate boards", by Professor Boris Groysberg, Harvard Business School, January 2013.

established their core group, they do develop something of a boys' club. I am aware that I could be criticised on this point and would like to emphasise it's just an opinion I hold. Take, for example, the famous Garrick Club in London which only recently voted no to allowing women as members. When the Guardian newspaper asked one of the club's members why they were objecting to women, they said the following:

"Men behave differently if there are no women there. There is camaraderie, banter... the knowledge that you can say anything you want and have a jolly good discussion about anything in a completely egalitarian atmosphere in which no one is trying to impress anyone else. That's my main objection to having women members – it's not against women, but the idea that some men would not be able to resist showing off to impress the women, that is an innate male characteristic, whether you are a bird or an animal. At the moment, any sort of pomposity or self-importance is punctured. You don't need to show off, you can be yourself, have uninhibited conversation, indulge in flights of fantasy. Having women members would change the nature of the club."[48]

There are of course women only network groups/ organisations, much for the same purpose as articulated

---

[48] http://www.theguardian.com/world/2015/jul/06/garrick-club-votes-to-continue-with-ban-on-women-members. The article on 6th July 2015 reported that 50.5% of members voted for women to be allowed as members but the club requires a two-thirds majority before rules can be changed.

above; and then there are organisations globally that create women only groups within their organisations to offer support, guidance and growth.

My question is – by having different networking groups based on gender, are we missing something? In my position as managing director of a law firm, 85% of the clients/ business associates with whom I network are male. If I exclude myself from the male community I fear I would miss out on the next business opportunity. I suspect that my male counterparts see it differently and have an easier way of bonding with other men. Clearly substantive research is needed in this area to do it justice. But is the business world or society as a whole even remotely interested if we network differently and is it happy with separate networking groups?

To find out, I have attempted to address this with the people I have interviewed for the book, but there was a lack of acceptance amongst my interviewees that there are any differences between the genders or changes in behaviour overall.

That being said, the interviews do provide a good insight into how others perceive and approach networking. My interviewees also offer lots of advice and tips on how to do it well. The gender difference issue was avoided as a whole and perhaps a more in-depth consideration of this particular topic will be revisited at another time.

Enjoy!

The interviews

I have interviewed a variety of men and women who are at different stages of their careers. Some have completed a question and answer session, some have responded to questions and others simply allowed me to interview them. Some of my respondents have asked to remain anonymous.

 **The men**

Eddie Davies BSc (Hons) MSc MAPM FRICS, Operations Director, MAMG

How important is face to face networking?

For many businesses, face to face networking is the bottom line. Without visibility, getting contacts and creating relationships, the opportunities themselves will not appear. We do business with people. A client will enter into a contract with your company based on your people and their skills, without which systems and technology are meaningless. Clients will appoint those they:

    like

    trust

🔖 consider value for money.

Trust depends on credentials, shared history and reputation. Value for money is often dictated by the market alongside a person's ability, efficiency and perceived 'values'. But how can they like you, without the ability to meet you face to face? Similarly, trust can be improved by the impression you leave.

At each stage of a tender such face to face moments help shortlisting, through an interview and final selection. In a tightly contested situation, a client may have two bids; both are a good price, good CVs, experience, etc. You may be finally selected because you recently met - it could be that simple and that important.

What works for you?

Through networking one hopes to create relationships that become opportunities, but the focus must be to make friends and hopefully create a lasting connection. This should not be a contrived manipulation of acquaintances, but enjoying people's company and creating honest rapport.

Any tips/words of wisdom?

Rashmi always encourages me (whether she realises it or not) to be myself - not that I'm a wallflower. So, on the assumption that you have an engaging personality, be assured in your opinions and predilections, obviously assuming that you do not become too outrageous or offensive, or too dull, e.g. talking about your geranium collection. That's a secret, by the way, don't tell anyone! Avoid being seen as a desperate networker, chasing around a room like a wee annoying Scottish midge.[49] I have made that mistake in the past. Yes, you're there to mix, but also to create rapport, to create interest, to bring value.

At events where alcohol is readily available, keep alert, don't lean in and smother, never get as drunk as your client, etc. In fact, you should be able to mix, talk and be engaging without alcohol. We have all made that mistake, but just keep an eye on it. Remember everyone is different. Not all will appreciate your drinking exploits, although some may be more relaxed with a pint.

We need to be broad and complex enough for conversation to flow naturally. This is not contrived manipulation, but we should find life in all its colour, its light and shade, interesting. We should be broad in our interests and thoughtful in our considerations.

Do you think men and women network differently?

We are social creatures, and men and women, stereotypically, have different interests or perspectives. However, putting social norms of how to greet one another and how to banter etc to one side, whether male or female, we simply want to create rapport. We seek to be open,

---

[49] I should point out Eddie is Scottish – from Glasgow, UK.

honest, engaging and intelligent. We seek to communicate passion and commitment generally, as well as relating to our profession.

My own experience as a man, is that it (having women present) is usually better, as a generalisation. It often adds an extra dynamic to trigger conversation and create rapport and, often, a different and helpful perspective, helping to respond to nuances of conversation and to turn conversation. Amongst men, a woman can sometimes interject in a way a man in a group wouldn't, often with humour and/or insight.

What are your views on networking using social media – is there a place for this?

Social networking is important for your general profile. Whether it is appropriate to mix personal and professional is debatable. There is a place for it where you are selling services, involving personal or corporate reputation (compared to selling products), and some courage is needed to put your personality on display, but in a competitive environment you need to set yourself apart. This needs initially a little courage and self-belief.

Do you have a networking story or experience you would like to share?

There is no question, even in the relatively small community in which I specialise that networking events always create a contact that you don't expect. On several occasions, over the years, an introduction at an event has triggered or led to commissions for me and my team and a lasting connection with the individuals involved. It may seem lucky or random, but I would disagree. Better to consider such occasions and subsequent turn of events as prescient, as springboards, which have been created through our engagement with the world around us.

Andrew Jackson, Head of Collections & Recoveries at Funding Circle. Andrew was a solicitor in private practice in the City of London for nine years before he joined Funding Circle in 2013.

How important is face to face networking?

Face to face networking is the best. Networking is about communicating clearly, and the more information we have to help us communicate the better. By face to face networking we can pick up body language as well as aural information, which all helps to manoeuvre a keen networker from failure to success.

What works for you?

When I was in private practice I was a 'seller'. I would engage in networking by being enthusiastic and curious, but mostly it was a waste of time because I was too early in my career to impact the more senior 'work-givers'. Also I didn't have enough experience about industry or business in general to be a convincing expert for those at the same level as me. I knew the law, but business acumen comes from experience which cannot be learnt. This became frustrating and so I went to networking events to simply enjoy myself, in the hope that I might get future work by gaining friends along the way.

Now that I am a buyer, I network to discuss commercial issues and be challenged on the unique practices of my team, and to find out whether there are innovations out there that I want to adopt. In other words, it is either for promotion of my team or information to help us innovate - I am not interested in being sold to. If I am in a networking scenario and it turns 'social' I usually steer it back to business as I have enough friends to be social with, and there is limited time in which I want to network.

Any tips?

Good networking creates a 'first date' feeling of excitement. Both parties feel that they are sharing enthusiasm, knowledge and interest, and are looking forward to their next meeting. For the person networking, it is important for them to keep in mind at all times their main purpose:

- Is it to win work?

- Is it to create further introductions?

- Is it to learn about an industry, product, person or innovation?

- Is it to build profile in the industry?

At networking environments, not everyone will have one of these four purposes in mind. These people are dead-ducks, and can be a waste of time for the keen networker. They are in that environment solely to:

- enjoy the free event, and/or free drinks and food, or

- see their current contacts or old friends.

These people should be avoided.

Do you think men and women network differently? If so how?

Yes, but only to the extent that men and women behave differently to other men and women in normal social situations. It is, in my view, dangerous to generalise by gender, although social stereotypes may give us insight into different styles, rather than substance.

Do you find it easier, harder or indifferent when networking with women?

I am indifferent - it makes no difference when both parties

are aligned in their understanding that the reason for the communication is purely networking. There must be an authentic interest to engage in an efficient exchange of information.

What are your views on networking using social media – is there a place for this?

Technology is accelerating and expanding our ability to communicate with other people, for better or for worse. With every new channel of communication there is a new opportunity for networking and business facilitation. LinkedIn is great for keeping in contact with business colleagues but Facebook is for friends only.

Do you have a networking story or experience you would like to share?

I was once advised that you had to kiss a lot of frogs to meet your prince. I found it arrogant and condescending to suggest that human relationships are simply a numbers game. It should not be about numbers, but it should be about effectiveness.

Done well, networking is the art of communication. You need to choose your targets carefully and make it count if you are not to waste time and energy. As a general rule:

- Between strangers, networking is about making an immediate connection that creates trust and value.

- Between acquaintances it is about reinforcing trust and finding a commonality of values.

- Between friends it is about helping each other to deal with problems and succeed in business.

Calvin Dexter, financial and property broker

How important is face to face networking?

I see it as a vital part of business development. It is self-marketing, by being in front of people you become visible and you jog people's memories. It is a promotion, a showcase of yourself, which often leads to opportunities.

What works for you?

I am very comfortable within myself. I have always taken pride in my appearance and see it as part of my personal brand – it is almost my 'calling card' – three-piece suit and a handkerchief in the top right hand pocket. I now know a lot of people and have good relationships with them. So now it is easier for me to ask them to introduce me to people I should know.

When I was starting out and was new to the world of

networking, but also new in my profession of finance, I would literally attend the opening of an envelope. Looking back, I made as many connections as possible because at that time it was very hard to know who you should be connecting with, particularly as you grow within yourself and your profession. I now see that I did use a scattergun approach in the early days but I was finding my feet. It took me 12 months to work and build connections; it may take longer for some people. I was lucky in that I was relatively outgoing as an individual. Now I work with my close connections and am continuously on the lookout to build new relationships but am more strategic in my approach and with my time.

Once you start talking to someone and find out more about them, ask yourself, do they add value to me? I would say it is the follow up that is very important. Exchange business cards, and if you think there is a business relationship to be had with the person follow up with a call and make an appointment to go and see them. So for example I recently attended an accountant's dinner and was introduced to someone who represented incremental value. I took their business card because once back in the office it acts a prompt to contact that person and follow up. I sometimes write a note on the card to remind me of, say, a sporting interest/something that we have in common.

Any tips?

It is important to establish why you are attending an event; is it to establish yourself in the market and/or to get contacts? Before the event get an attendees list or list of exhibitors who are attending and think about who you should be targeting. Also see people that you know to catch up with, remember it is about being in front of them and reminding them of you. Ensure you follow up. Even if you wanted to see someone on the list that you were unable to meet, drop them a line saying "sorry, I wanted to meet up with you but was unable to do so" and try and arrange for a coffee. Try and get people you know to help facilitate introductions; it is easier and known as a warm introduction – people will be more willing to give you their time.

It is sometimes easier to have an interest in something outside of work. For me I like sports and I am a very keen golfer. This sometimes helps me break the ice in conversations. The small talk can be just as important. This is also when you must have very good listening skills and have an open technique when in conversation with others. I spend a lot of time listening to what others have to say.

Do men and women network differently?

I believe that men have more confidence as they find it easier to be in a room predominantly full of men. I believe that some women get intimidated by a room that is 95% full of men and find it harder to infiltrate group discussions.

There are differences in the way men and women network and how they approach conversations, I don't think it is easier or different to network with women; from my perspective I am the same. I think when you are younger it is also different. Being in your 20's for example, you will naturally gravitate towards younger professionals, as you can feel intimidated by older and more experienced professionals. At this age you can build confidence by engaging with a similar age peer group.

What are your views on networking using social media – does it have a place?

Yes it does. It adds value, but you can never lose the face to face. Things like Twitter, LinkedIn and blogs are good for keeping in touch with people.

Do you have a networking story or experience you would like to share?

I started working at Cattles in 2001 in business development for East & South Yorkshire; I had never worked in the industry before. I regularly attended the Sheffield Business Club to get to know people. I asked to be introduced to someone who I wanted to do business with. We met up and during our conversation I discovered that we both had a love for golf and that he was a member of a club where I was about to join. Most of the night's conversation was on golf and very little on business. The person I met that night became and remains a very good friend and we have done a lot of business together over the years on and off the golf course. Networking is about building relationships, which over time will create value. If I had a message it would be:

1. Know your personal brand

2. Ask for introductions to other people

3. Find people you want to build relationships with

4. Aim for groups that have a common interest.

5. Ensure that you follow up.

Leo de Montaignac, CEO, Weedingtech[50]

How important is face to face networking?

Face to face is very important in business. People invest in people and face to face conversation is an important part of that; it allows one to build a relationship that is long term. Relationship building is a slow burn. You cannot just go into the pitch - you have to build the relationship. A pitch in itself can be tedious, and people really do also want a long term working relationship with people, they want a relationship that lasts a long time. Face to face networking therefore is

---

[50] Weeding Technologies Limited.

invaluable. I don't think it can be replaced.

Do you have any tips/advice?

Don't be afraid to speak to people and tell them what you are looking for. What is the worst that can happen, is my theory. If you are at the beginning of your career don't worry about speaking to people, just try it as you have nothing to lose and everything to gain. You may be nervous but show interest in the other person, take time to listen to them and build a connection. Listening to others and understanding them is a vital part to building a relationship. Ask questions about them and build confidence within yourself and the relationship you are building. It's about listening and taking your time over the relationship.

Do you think men and women network differently?

I don't see men and women networking differently. Men may approach a situation differently and possibly a little egotistically and make an assumption that the deal is done. While women, I find, have an approach towards relationship building which I find works the best in the long term. Equally I do not approach women any differently to men when networking, the objective for me is to build relationships that are long lasting.

Do you think social networking is affecting face to face networking?

Face to face networking is invaluable and cannot be replaced with social networking. Social networking has a place, and acts as a complement to the face to face, but it is, when broken down, about relationships that last a long time and doing business with people you like. There is a place and requirement for social media, it can make people more aware of you and your product or service but they will need to still speak to you and will still want to know who you are as a person.

Do you have story or experience you would like to share to illustrate the importance of networking?

I belong to a members club, where friends introduce me to other people. This is a great place to build relationships with people. You spend time understanding them and you both get to know each other. You share and discuss business but you are not pitching! Over time and building personal connections and relationships, I was eventually introduced to an investor, who did later invest in the business. Networking is always to me about building relationships based upon understanding and knowing the person on personal matters as well as professional.

Gareth Boot, Managing Director of The PIC Group

In the interview with Gareth, I did ask questions as I have of the others but took a more fluid approach. I had only met Gareth recently in Yorkshire at a private event. During my conversation with him he came across as an expert in his field, very relaxed and very confident and comfortable networking. At a subsequent meeting (the follow up) I discovered that Gareth is very nervous about networking to the point where it makes him physically ill. But he understands the need and the requirement for networking so has learnt to overcome his fears and anxiety.

Are you naturally just shy or is it more about insecurities? How does it manifest itself and why do you choose to put yourself through the networking experience?

I think it stems from when I was younger; I was very skinny, with red hair and I was picked upon. In terms of having to network, I was forced to attend seminars and events when I started my career in the motor car industry. I was almost forced to meet people because it was part of the job. I remember before the events – starting a week before not just the night before - I would start feeling sick, nausea would set in and I would vomit. It wasn't pleasant. However the ironic thing is when I attended the events I loved meeting the people, and used to leave the events feeling on a natural high and fantastic and people would comment on how confident and self-assured I seemed.

My journey began in 1994. Over the next 10 years I continued along the same path, discovering and working out the reason I was networking as a salesman in the motor industry. This was down to two reasons:

- pro-selling

- getting to know people, both suppliers and clients.

I also learnt that instant gratification in terms of quick business turnaround was not a healthy way of conducting business. Establishing long-lasting relationships was better. It was not about getting as many business cards as possible without creating a rapport with the people I met.

From 2006 things stepped up a gear in that I became self-employed and therefore chose to go out to network. I had developed my confidence, but still had the same nerves before an event. So, for instance, at a recent Yorkshire Mafia meeting I was nervous about going, thinking there will be people there who are more confident than me, look better, but I knew that a friend of mine, "Bob", was going to be there and he had already talked to me about Rashmi. My confidence was good and I was controlling my nerves using the NLP[51] training I had undertaken. However I became very nervous and anxious about the event when I got a message from Bob to say that he was going to be late. However, I still

---

[51] Neuro-linguistic programming.

overcome them and attended the event, which I enjoyed and developed further relationships with people.

What tips/advice can you offer?

1. Get to know the person you are speaking to. Try and find some common ground. When I met Rashmi she made it easy for me to talk to her and we soon found the common ground of cricket, both of us being fans.

2. Face to face networking is always the best as it helps develop relationships.

3. Always speak to people. I purchased my business simply by speaking to the owner in a car park!

4. It's ok to be nervous and shy, but you have to come up with your own ways of overcoming that. In today's environment whether you are an employee or business owner, you have to network to build your profile and to create your own client and supplier base.

The women

Years ago, I was on my way to a networking event and I got a call from a colleague who was already there, concerned she had gone to the wrong place. I checked where she was and it was the right location. I informed her I was just parking the car and would be with her shortly. When I met her she was waiting outside the hotel where the event was taking place, I asked why she was worried. She told me: "Everyone else here is a man." I entered the hotel room and had a look around, although there were a few women, most of the other attendees were indeed men.

This had thrown my colleague who was quite young at the time as she a) assumed that the event was for women and b) was not sure how she should interact. I explained that it was a 'mixed' event and just treat them the same as women – there was nothing to be fearful of. However it did dawn on me at that moment perhaps that is why men will notice women and what they are wearing – they're so used to seeing men that women are a breath of fresh air.

However, the shoe was on the other foot with me when I attended an event in London where there were 68 men and me. Yes it was a mixed event but it turned out that women had not attended because they'd been told it was an event solely attended by men. When I tell this story to women, they always ask me if that made me nervous but it didn't – in fact I loved it! The only problem it gave me was remembering all the attendees' names while it was easy for them to remember mine - I was the only lady in the room! But of course, I was in a fortunate position: my message was going to get out!

I can understand why being the only woman in that situation might make you feel nervous but just don't think of them as men. Someone once told me, it's not how many men or women are in the room, it's how many brains there are.

In these interviews I speak to women about their experiences and views on networking.

This interviewee wished to remain anonymous.

How important is face to face networking?

I find face to face networking extremely important. I am able to read a situation and a person's reaction far better when I meet them face to face. I believe communication goes beyond written or spoken words; and so meeting in person allows relationships to develop quicker through the other tools of communication - for example, through humour.

Meeting face to face is a chance to present yourself smartly; often I find that physical appearance shapes my opinion of someone, especially at a first impression. Face to face networking allows you to judge better the progression of a conversation, to assess the other person's engagement as well as their interest in you and in the topic of conversation. These social cues allow you to adapt your approach or conversation to better suit the other person and their interests.

Often people remember a face but not a name - and even names change often, for example through marriage. Meeting face to face thus gives a better chance for recognition and lets the all-too-common phrase "where have I met you before?" to come out and trigger an interaction. This can allow two people to recall places, meetings or colleagues in common. I also find, particularly in the role of an expert, that meeting face to face enables you to demonstrate or to assess someone's confidence and presence, and observe first-hand how memorable and convincing they are. Confidence appears in the volume and tone of voice, in posture, in an introduction, and in a handshake.

The enhanced communication aspects of face to face

networking make it essential in an international world. Although someone may not completely understand my words (either because of language barriers or mannerisms such as sarcasm), my smile can swiftly communicate to them that I mean well or that I am joking. It is easier to put someone at ease, and easier to assess how they wish to communicate with you. In the Middle East for instance, it is of utmost importance to wait until someone offers to shake your hand. In Asia, it is essential to show respect by bowing the head and exchanging business cards with both hands, whilst reading them carefully.

What works for you?

I do prefer face to face meetings, but the format of the meeting depends very much on who I am meeting, what their religion/culture is, and how well I know them. I prefer to arrange more formal and shorter introductions with people I have never met before. I am more than happy to meet people I have known for a long time for an evening and perhaps for dinner. Building relationships takes time. As you get to know an individual and their interests, more and more meetings can be based around this knowledge, both educational and social. I also make sure that I help people as much as I can. I ask them how I can be of help and always look to arrange introductions or to let them know about events that may be of interest.

Any tips?

I know it sounds simple but the most important thing is to be a nice and approachable person who a client feels they can pick up the phone to, to be reliable and to try your best not to let people down unless it is completely unavoidable, and explain why if that happens. I also make sure that I maintain contact without hassling someone too much - after all we are all very busy. With international clients I endeavour to only contact them during their working hours, but I do try to reply to them even if it is not a work day for me.

Do you think men and women network differently? If so, how?

I really haven't noticed a difference; I think it's more about the way different personalities network rather than men and women. Within my team, I encourage people to network in a way that suits them. Some excel at giving formal seminars, some are best in small groups over dinner or lunch, while others are excellent at getting around a room full of people.

Do you find it easier, harder or no different when networking with women?

Personally I find it easier with men, or with strong women (of which there are many in the construction industry). I was one of a few girls admitted to an all-boys school in sixth form, went on to study civil engineering in a male dominated environment, and now work with mostly men. Funnily enough most of my friends are also male. The females that I get on well with are all strong, professional women with a similar approach to life as myself. They avoid gossip, unnecessary emotions and are very straight talkers.

What are your views on networking using social media – does it have a place?

There is most definitely a place for this. It is, however, usually once you know someone or a group better. It often works to chat to a client about things other than work, to give them an enjoyable evening - be it golf, a drink, or dinner. Usually I make sure that the discussion about how we can work together is done separately in a more formal business environment.

Tracy Fletcher, Managing Director of Campbell and Fletcher

How important is face to face networking?

Vital. Building relationships is the most important part of networking. Before asking for business, establish a solid relationship based on mutual respect. The best way to build the relationship is face to face as it is more personable. When you are face to face you are able to pick up on nuances - body language, facial expressions, eye contact, mirroring their behaviour and genuinely being interested in who they are - these are all part of building the relationship. The art of networking is not going in for the deal.

What works for you?

The issue with or around poor return is not having an outcome in mind, it is not having or taking the time to get to know the individual before asking them for business or for them to get to know you. Networking is an Art not a science - what is important is not to use someone else's way of networking or try and approach it in a formulaic way, it's all about who you are and your personality. Science is a process, Art is intuition, perception, observation and listening - there is no game plan.

I try to establish common ground quickly. This is when it is useful to have your own interest and hobbies outside the working environment, so you can relate to people. I am not a golfer but I am well read, and I enjoy running. I can talk comfortably without any pretence on a variety of subjects. It is important to be business-like and understand the outcome. Learn to read the signs - when is it right to develop the conversation into a more business-like manner? You cannot pitch until they are ready to hear it. The buyer and seller's values have to be aligned.

Any tips?

- Be genuine.

- Don't rush it, take your time.

- Don't push.

Do you find it easier, harder or no different when networking with women?

There is too much of an expectation on men and women to act differently. There is a lot of talk that men and women network differently, which can lead to expectation and ultimately becomes a self-fulling prophecy. I am not an advocate of women-only networking but am an advocate of Women in Business. The best networking events I have been to have mixed men and women networking together. Fundamentally, the networking is different because we are different. I'd qualify this by saying I think there is more expectation of men to ask for business. I will try not to generalise but with men once business is out of the way they will relax and socialise while women develop a relationship before they conduct a transaction. It is ok to be different because it is worse when we are not – it goes back to being genuine.

What are your views on networking using social media – does it have a place?

Yes, it's absolutely vital to embrace all current technology. It is not a substitute for face to face networking but it can be used to demonstrate your brand knowledge and expertise to your peers and clients.

Do you have story or experience you would like to share to illustrate the importance of networking?

I was unable to obtain a ticket to an event that is very big in my industry, however the bar area where people went to after the event was open and so I went to the bar where I networked and met my first big client for my business.

Amanda Lennon, Founding Partner, Innov8tive Minds Ltd

This interview was less structured, but it provides an insight into where most people sit in terms of networking, that is to say, we don't particularly like to network and it is out of our comfort zone, no matter how long we have been doing it. However the thing about Amanda is she is a very well 'networked' individual and makes it seem so very easy. She has always come across as authentic/real and personable.

What do you think of networking?

I hate networking, and yes I am fully aware of the word I'm using. For those people that pay attention to psychometric testing I'm actually an introvert, no one ever believes that, but I find people and social situations really quite draining. I learnt to be more extroverted when I was a teenager. Networking is hugely important to my business and while I do have to make an effort to put on my 'game face' and prepare, I do also make sure that I am not disingenuous but am still me. I just present a more sociable version of me!

Does your attire make a difference or should it even be considered?

I always consider what I wear. My work requires me to connect with all manner of people – academics, politicians, civil servants, business leaders, entrepreneurs, developers and coders – all sorts! I am a firm believer in the power of non-verbal communication and think that clothes play an important part in that. So, for instance, when I am meeting developers I might wear jeans, but when meeting clients perhaps a dress and heels. I see both as my uniform given that my natural attire is incredibly scruffy!

What tips do you have?

Be authentic, a fraud is always spotted and there is no second chance for a first impression! Project an impression of who you really are (even if like me it's simply a more sociable version of you) but don't mismanage expectations or present something that you're really not. Listen more than you talk but relax – everyone is human – this is meant to be fun as much as it is useful.

Do you have a story to share about networking?

Charlie, my son, is 20 and a 6ft 2inch rugby lad. I've taken him to events for years, I think the first time he attended an event with me he was about 13 years old. He always appears completely comfortable in any environment, he will talk to anyone – and he's met some really interesting people – rocket scientists, the retired Head of Russian Mission Control, David Cameron – again all sorts of folks! While he is sometimes daunted, his attitude is very much, "but they're all just people – what is there to be worried about?"

Men, women and networking – any comments or observations?

I think we've all been in situations where one party (male or female) has been perhaps a little too familiar and this is sometimes simply as a result of the blurring of social and business lines (often as a result of alcohol!). As the mother of a daughter I'm often considering how to explain the need to be sensitive to environments and advances but in a business networking environment I think these situations are generally easy to handle. With regard to female-only events, despite being a 'card carrying feminist', I generally have a dim view of these. As women we have to deal with men in business and in life, if we segregate ourselves or demand different standards, then surely we're undermining our own ability and almost discriminating against ourselves, if that makes sense.

The final two interviews are with people who run networking organisations and arrange networking events. I thought it would he beneficial to get their perspectives on the matter.

Griselda Togobo, Owner and Managing Director of Forward Ladies

Why have a women only networking organisation?

Forward Ladies was formed out of a need for women to come together to network and support each other. The organisation responded to that need which resulted in its growth over the past 16 years. Some women do not enjoy networking in mixed gender networks. They find it intimidating and prefer to network with other women in more informal and relaxed setting.

Is there a demand for men only networking groups?

There is no demand for men's only networking groups as the status quo favours men. There are a lot more men in the business world and in high positions which makes it easier for them to dictate the way events are organised. Traditionally men have also used opportunities at pubs or golf days to network. With all these opportunities to network, it's not surprising that there is no demand for men only networking groups.

Does or should maternity leave[52] affect networking?

You can still maintain a strong network even when you are on maternity leave. You have to remember that people are bound to move on to seek new and different opportunities but that does not mean you should lose contact with them. Staying in contact with people is a lot easier in today's connected world. You build and maintain a strong network, even if you rely heavily on social media.

I work hard on maintaining relationships by keeping in touch with people -even if only via social media. I use LinkedIn a lot and also organise to meet people whenever I can. Keeping in touch with work colleagues will make it easier to re-enter the workforce.

---

[52] At the time of writing, Griselda was on maternity leave.

What are your views on networking?

When I first started networking I hated it. I still hate those 60 second pitches at breakfast meetings where it's basically a sales pitch and it's driven by a focus on sales and not relationships. I prefer networking where the focus in on building relationships. It is still very difficult for me when I find I am the only female in the room but I am quite happy to use that to my advantage because I will stand out in the room.

The positives of networking I find are extraordinary because it's amazing how many people you can meet and establish lasting relationships with. Through networking you can meet mentors and create business opportunities. I think networking with the right people can also change your perspective on life and influence you both professionally and personally.

Any tips?

Networking is an opportunity to meet and gain access to some fantastic connections with the view of helping people and supporting them as well as building relationships. Do not approach it with the mentality of "what can I get out of these people?" You need to approach it with the intention to give first.

Always be yourself. Be authentic. This will help you build rapport and trust quicker.

Be interested in people and follow up after making contact with them.

Social media and networking - does it have a place?

Social media is fantastic! It's even more powerful when used in conjunction with face to face meetings. Social media is a great way to connect with people and can bring huge opportunities. Social media platforms such as LinkedIn, Twitter and Facebook are useful for sharing content and over time you'll establish yourself as a thought leader or expert based on whatever content you share. You'll be amazed how many people read your content and begin to feel that they know you. It is a great opportunity to build your profile. Make the most of it.

Geoff Shepherd, Chairman, Yorkshire Mafia

What is your view on networking?

I avoided it for most of my (to date) professional life. I guess that I saw it largely as the dark art of the desperate circling the needy. To some degree that's probably still true, especially of those events where you meet the business card before you meet the person holding it. Through running my own event I've learnt that I enjoy unstructured and informal networking. It's expanded my circling of suppliers, customers, advisors and friends. There's little to lose, everyone should give it a go and find a format that works for them and their business.

Do you think men and women network differently?

Yes. Women tend to be much better at it! The evidence is anecdotal but women seem to be more natural, collegiate and open.

What tips do you have for face to face networking?

Listen, be respectful, ask questions, don't interrupt a group of people who are talking, don't try and sell anything, follow up any actions over the following day or two, be yourself and try to have fun.

You started an online community - Yorkshire Mafia Group on LinkedIn. How do you see the role of social media in terms of networking?

Largely as an accelerator and coordination tool. LinkedIn allowed us to amass a groundswell of support quickly and communicate directly with that membership.

Why organise women only events? Do the men object?

Some do, some don't. Like most things, it's down to personal perspective. Some women are more comfortable in a female-only environment and that should be respected. Ultimately, people vote with their feet. If it wasn't wanted, no one would attend.

Would you like a share a story about networking that you have experienced?

I'm not sure that I have a one-off story about networking. There have been many instances of friendships struck, relationships built, old acquaintances rekindled and so on. About half of my business turnover originates from our networking efforts. I met many of my friends at our events, most of my suppliers were met through The Yorkshire Mafia. It's been a tremendous success story for me, both professionally and personally. I've gained business directly and indirectly, I've founded joint ventures, met our now non-exec director. With fellow Yorkshire Mafia members, I've been to Morocco, Tanzania, cycled to Paris (from Leeds) twice, and much more. I've used it to build one of the biggest business events in the country and to generate tens of millions in revenue for the local economy. Lifelong friendships, better business, more revenue and exploring the world with friends; networking... I'm pretty pleased that I finally got around to it!

Chapter 9

Networking for newbies

"Don't let fear or insecurity stop you from trying new things. Believe in yourself. Do what you love. And most importantly, be kind to others, even if you don't like them." Stacy London[53]

"Smile, for everyone lacks self-confidence and more than any other one thing a smile reassures them." André Maurois[54]

You can be a newbie at any age, at any point of your career – you are simply 'new' to networking. But if you are just starting out - as a new employee, as an apprentice, as a

---

[53] An American stylist/fashion consultant, author, and magazine editor.

[54] French author.

graduate - networking can feel even more daunting. It's not, after all, something they teach in school! Having given lectures to students and postgraduates on networking, I want to share, in this chapter, my tips on finding your way of doing it.

Shall we begin? The water is lovely! Grab your tools – armbands, rubber rings, and don't forget your swimsuit! Now dive in or tiptoe in – either way come and join the party.

Maybe it is easier to not think of it as networking but as collaborating? Let's take a TV show for example. The writers, producers, actors, hair and makeup artists, special effects teams and many more, who are usually all self-employed and could be just starting out in the industry or be well-established - they all have to collaborate with each other in order to bring a production together. Effectively, they are networking with each other for that particular project. Plus, as they are self-employed, they then have to ensure they continue to network, by maintaining those relationships and building new ones. The individual self-employed person does not have an army of people to send out and network for them. Their roles/positions are largely based on how well they network as well as their individual talent.

Still studying?

Even if you're studying and have not yet entered the world of work, it's never too early to start networking. Earlier, I used the example of the postgraduates in law I met who were trying to build contacts with law firms and asked to come networking with me. It was good practise for them and they made a lot of good connections. It is also advisable to get guidance from your teachers and lecturers. Stay in contact with them – I have had lecturers recommend students to me, from within their network. I know of a student who completed her postgraduate course in law, but was struggling to find a position within a law firm, or to secure any form of paralegal work. As a result of staying connected with her lecturers she secured a paralegal position, which in turn led to a training contract. Keep in touch with your fellow students too – they could be in a position to offer you assistance in the future. Or, of course, you might be able to help them.

As a student it is important to attend events that are relevant to the industry you're in. It can be useful to call event organisers beforehand and explain you are a student - you might get a discount and they may be able to recommend other useful networking opportunities.

Just started working?

Starting out in any industry, you often just want to get your head down and ensure you are doing a good job. That is of course vital but equally important is understanding the need to network within your industry. Businesses nowadays are becoming more demanding. They want more than someone at their desk doing the work – they want employees to have the ability and the skills to go out into the wider world and develop the business by building relationships, bridges and collaborations. Being able to network therefore is vital to your career.

The first place to start is within the company you are working for. Internal networking is really important when you are just starting out. But it can feel daunting to meet new people within your organisation. Start by finding out more about the people in your team and your department and see if there are social events that you can attend. Ask people for coffee in your organisation or seek out a mentor/ champion who can assist you in the development of your network.

A UK director of a global business once told me that a new junior member of staff had asked to have a coffee with him. He was extremely busy and did not have time, but knew how the other person would feel and how much they would benefit from that meeting so he arranged a coffee. From the newbie's perspective, he had started to build his contacts within the company, and would no doubt have benefited hugely from an hour's chat with the director. Of course, the director himself was also networking. Why? Well, it is just as important to build your network with those that are up and coming, if only to be a mentor, a person of guidance and support!

If you are self-employed – a writer working alone, for instance, or someone building a business with only one or two employees – find groups of people that you want to get to know. For example writers want to build relationships with publishers, journalists, presenters, producers and broadcasters. Find organisations or events where these people get together and start talking to them. There is no excuse not to start. You could even organise your own networking group, for example a regular social event.

But, we do often make excuses, don't we?! "I have so much work on my desk which needs to be completed. How can I be expected to network as well? What does my manager/ boss expect of me?" The key to this is to remember that networking will benefit you in the long run, you will develop your skills, increase your contacts within your industry and build your credibility.

Most people in business need to build external as well as internal networks. So how would you explore the external world? Look up events and ask people which events they go to. Why do they like them? Remember, there's a difference between simply liking an event and liking an event that will be beneficial. At some point, you will no doubt get invited to a breakfast morning networking group, where a group of local business people meet to discuss business and try to help each out in some way. They provide excellent opportunities to learn how to to 'mingle' and to practise speaking publicly, as often at these events you will have a slot in which you can tell people about your business using, what we called earlier, your 'elevator pitch'. Once you meet people, use the opportunity to invite them to connect on LinkedIn. Remember - always make the invitation personal and remind them where you met.

When I first started out, I often felt like I would attend the opening of an envelope! But it was important for me at that stage in my career to get my face, name and message out there. This proved very effective when I first started in business, but as I developed, expanded and grew, I've become much more selective in terms of the events I attend. I need to be clear that they are the right events for me and my business. Otherwise the risk is that my brand and Legatus Law's brand become diluted. I therefore make sure that we are targeted in the events we attend and that it is people from my construction and engineering team that attend that particular industry's events, while others in the mergers and acquisitions team attend events with private equity firms, for instance.

If you are of the older generation, you may believe you know a thing or two about networking. I visited Leeds Law School to do a presentation on networking to postgraduates. There were a number of mature students in attendance who had some awareness of the industry. It was interesting to gauge their reactions. Their questions mainly centred on issues of how to get in front of people. What they had yet to realise is that it is not just about getting out there, it is about the follow up conversion and without that you can be at a loss.

Once you have met the people that you wish to focus on and want to develop a relationship with, it is essential to make a list of their names. As I have said previously it is all about building relationships and then considering what you can bring to the table - to strengthen that relationship and connection. Plus, I've found that, in most cases, people will want to help me too, because it is the right thing to do.

Go on, make a splash! What have you got to be worried about?

Chapter 10

Networking at work

"Being happy outside the pool means fast swimming in the pool." Eric Shanteau[55]

This chapter overlaps with other chapters where I have already discussed the importance of networking internally. However, because this is so important I wanted to dedicate a specific chapter to it.

Working in larger organisations you will be surrounded by people. Often you will only know and associate with your team. The more senior you become the more people you will get to know. Obviously, if you move from one department to another you will widen the pool of people you know (don't

---

[55] Eric Lee Shanteau is an American former competition swimmer who won two gold medals as a member of winning United States relay teams at the World Championships.

forget, though, to stay connected with your old contacts while developing your new contacts).

For me, internal networking helps support:

1. The day to day/operational side of working life

2. Your personal development.

Operational

This could be when you are moving within the company from, say, a manager to a more leadership role, or perhaps becoming regional director or growing your business. The default position is wanting to get your head down and do an excellent job, be recognised and move ahead. We can become unsettled and uneasy sometimes when we have moved into a new arena, trying to understand our new roles and do them well. We might believe that we have to do this alone. That is not the case. Networking internally provides both support and vision.

There is a perception that networking within the corporation you work for is 'brown-nosing'. But this is not the case. It will help you to understand the direction the business is taking and therefore filters down into how you manage your team. This helps with strategic growth and building strong relationships. It is important, I would say vital, to ensure that you network outside the immediate circle of your team with more senior members of staff. This would include senior directors, board members and stakeholders. This will help you plan for the future with your team and predict changes within the business.

Personal Development

The other advantage of networking within your company is that it can help with your own personal and professional development. An illustration of this might be building a relationship with maybe a non-executive director who could help you develop, by either mentoring you or introducing you to an external network of people. You might think you don't have the time for this. Why spend the time with people who you feel will not further your career? This is because it is all about relationships and building contacts. A personal network of people helps provide support and develops our day to day skills within our chosen vocation.

Having spoken to a number of people working in larger organisations the general consensus is being able to perform or deliver is really a given. Gone are the days where if you worked hard that was all you needed to do to be recognised and promoted. These days, a little something extra is required. You do need to widen your horizons and build your network, not just within your region or division but with the wider organisation. This will help you understand different leadership styles, what the other parts of the organisation are thinking and their objectives which can be fed back to your team/division to see how it all fits into the whole picture. The key aspects you should focus on are:

1. Deliver – perform

2. Build your relationships within the business/department/team

3. Build your relationships with other managers, stakeholders and networks within the organisation.

Sometimes you come up against internal politics. There might be people in the organisation who are an important part of the business and who your section cannot do without. They may not be part of the team but in order to obtain results you need their assistance. You may have to spend a fair amount of time with these people and, if you are lucky, you will get to know them and like them. However there may be instances where this is not the case, it's not that you dislike them but you may not become friends. This is ok. The important aspect is to be authentic, genuine in the relationships you build.

Building relationships is hard, you need to be aware of people's body language, the silent signals and messages they give. In some instances you may have to manage difficult egos, or conflict. Sometimes people may just not get along with you. Yes, it is a minefield but internal networking is a vital part of the day to day job.

Some organisations offer mentors which is a great way of getting support and guidance on how to manage relationships within the workplace but who can also help you to understand how to reach your next goal. If one is not provided ask someone you trust and get along with if they will mentor you.

Chapter 11

Why bother with networking?

"*I wouldn't say anything is impossible. I think that everything is possible as long as you put your mind to it and put the work and time into it.*" Michael Phelps[56]

"*People shouldn't look at me and think life is one big piece of glamour. That's the marketing, the spin. Life is challenging. But I have courage, strength, and enough good health to see the positive.*" Carmen Dell'Orefice[57]

---

[56] Michael Fred Phelps II is an American competition swimmer and the most decorated Olympian of all time, with a total of 22 medals in three Olympiads.

[57] Carmen Dell'Orefice is an American model and actress. She is known within the fashion industry for being the world's oldest working model as of the Spring/Summer 2012 season.

Reading this book, one could quite easily think that a lot of time and commitment is required to network. You might think, why should I bother? What do I gain?

Hopefully throughout the book I have highlighted the some of the benefits, but let's explore them a little more.

1. Self-confidence

By networking, you build your self-confidence about yourself and your expertise. Self-confidence in speaking and interacting with people has to be a positive and a good thing overall in your work and personal life. Networking also teaches you skills in understanding body language. By building your self-confidence you will develop a better understanding of yourself. There has been research[58] in this area that shows people with more belief in themselves and

---

[58] In October 2012, the University of Melbourne Business and Economics Division published a paper called *"Self-confidence - the secret to workplace advancement."* The findings showed upward mobility was more likely with people who had or 'faked' confidence. The overall conclusion was "that we should stress confidence-building activities at an early age. Such activities should be strongly encouraged both in formal schooling and within the family unit."

who portray self-confidence become more upwardly mobile.

2.   Contacts

Knowing people will always enhance you as a person. You will make a lot of connections with people who may become a very important part of your life whether in business or personally. Equally you could play an important role in someone else's life. The more people you know, the more you develop and the more you can help others.

3.   Support

Support through networking is a wonderful bi-product. You build close relationships with people and help support and nurture one another through your business and personal life. This might be through internal networking and mentoring. Alternatively it could be through an organisation that supports businesses, through networking and educational events. Sometimes , though, we might become so senior that we stop meeting new people - this is a good time to think outside the box, maybe by creating your own networking events!

4.   Friends

One of the best side effects of networking for me is meeting some amazing lovely people that have become friends, examples of which are laced through the book such as meeting someone at the start of a 10K run, or at a public appointments talk and simply being introduced to someone after a conference outside a pub at Westminster.

5.   Social

Have fun!!! Swimming is exercise but it can also be fun. Enjoy yourself, be social. But let us not forget that social also means media. It would be wrong to ignore a large part of how business operates. Use the internet and all it has to offer, but do not forget the face to face.

6.   Business

To help grow your business and/or career you cannot operate as an island; you will need the support of other businesses and other people. Build long term relationships of value.

7.   Mentoring

If you can get a mentor this will assist you and if you are already senior – help those that are climbing the ladder. *"If you're lucky enough to do well, it's your responsibility to send the elevator back down."* Kevin Spacey[59]

The thing about networking is it can be scary, daunting and nerve-racking, but think of it like swimming. Even if you can't swim, you'll always have fun. You might say "I am afraid of swimming." Well, we are all afraid of doing things we feel that we are not good at or don't know how to do, but really once we get in the pool we realise it's not that bad.

---

[59] Kevin Spacey Fowler CBE is an American actor, film director, producer, singer and comedian.

What you might discover is that the pool is smaller than you think – everyone is in the same place, just maybe at different stages. Just by doing it, you will learn to network and may even find that you enjoy it.

So dip your toe, jump or dive in but go on just do it and make a splash!

"Be you, be fabulous and have fun." Rashmi Dubé.

Appendix A

The art of networking in the digital age

(This article appeared in London Economic, March 2015)

In an age where children are born into the internet world, where most of us access numerous social media platforms at the click of a button – does digital networking work? If so, is there an art to it?

I have been an active networker for some time as an active member of business groups such as Forward Ladies which recognises, supports and connects women in business. I am also an active member of Turnaround Management Association (TMA). My membership of the groups have been incredibly worthwhile for me. I have been able to meet a number of people who have both served as useful contacts and some have become clients; I have won awards and have strengthened my profile in taking our collective views to

Parliament. But aside from the offline networking, especially in this digital age, what more is there a business owner can do?

I believe digital networking is now as important as face to face. This is because Facebook, Instagram, Twitter, LinkedIn and even emails use communications technology that I would describe as 'in your face'.

Most businesses want and need to be noticed, it is how we market ourselves and generate new business enquiries. And as a nation we're increasingly craving attention whether we are in business or personal – just ask yourself when the last time you took a selfie was? And, even if you didn't, when was the last time you saw one or heard about one? It has become a 'craze' that cannot be ignored. The same can be said of digital networking.

One of the big questions this prompts is this – with online socialising becoming such a quick way to network, do we actually need to meet any more? Social networking allows you an approach that is global and much farther reaching than just face to face. But the real art is the same as networking of any variety – knowing what it is you want to achieve and what your objective actually is?

If you are in business, this depends whether your business operates B2B or B2C and, in turn, establishing whether your messages are aimed at consumers or business people. One message does not fit all, one form of networking does not fit all.

Target your audience so that you know where they are. Will you find your next customer and community of support on Facebook, Twitter or LinkedIn? This will vary depending on the sector you are in, for example a friend of mine owns and runs a very successful pub and holds music events. LinkedIn, being a professional platform has not proven useful for his venture whereas Facebook and Twitter are his world.

You therefore need to use the appropriate platform to exhibit your value. Let others know you are an expert in your field and share knowledge to build credibility and become known as the go-to expert in your sector.

Personally I think LinkedIn is an invaluable source for business professional. It houses your CV and provides testimonials advising on your expertise. However I would not recommend spending all your networking time on LinkedIn as relationships are strengthened with face to face meetings. It can be the door opener you need, it cannot close the deal.

Critics analyse whether social media is an efficient way for business people to spend their time. The truth is most businesses today cannot afford not to be online. And with some experience, social networking can and should become a daily practice.

However, to answer my earlier question, it is not a replacement – face to face communication cannot be replaced. No matter how good you are, sitting in a room networking from your laptop, computer or even phone is not a substitute for a face to face meeting which allows the other person to get to you know on a different level. The conversation widens from a particular topic to weather, football, music and other pastimes, which in turn can strengthen a good relationship.

We live in a global marketplace which is more accessible than ever through online networking but the digital arena alone is just that – digital not real. It can help you identify your audience, communicate with them and start the process of engagement. But the real benefits will come when you convert that digital contact into a real life contact.

About the author

"Personality is the glitter that sends your little gleam across the footlights and the orchestra pit into that big black space where the audience is."
Mae West

Rashmi Dubé is the managing director of the multi-award-winning legal practice Legatus Law. She has been working in the legal profession for some 20 years, qualifying as a solicitor in England.

As well as being an expert business solicitor, lawyer and mediator, she is also a business mentor and dedicates time to charities.

Rashmi is recognised as a leading voice for the SME sector in the north of England, and is often invited to share her opinions on the BBC.

As a leading entrepreneur, Rashmi believes in the power of building genuine relationships. Drawing on her own experiences of networking, in her debut book she talks about the benefits and tools she uses to network successfully.

Acknowledgements

I would like to take some time to thank people for their support and wisdom over time and during the writing of this book.

The first people I have to thank are my parents Raj and Surya, for their love and support, Shailja Dubé and Dan Beatie for putting up with me saying for months/years, "I'm writing a book", Lynn Bassil for the guidance, Donald, Ed and Rick Nelson, for the constant guidance and unconditional love, Deborah Mills for saying "I can do it "when I suddenly realised that there were actual professional writers doing this thing daily as their job! My wonderful book club gals, Liz, Lisa, Rachel, Melissa, Dawn, Felicity, Jill, Jane, Yvonne and all the ladies I have forgotten to mention from the book club - a special thank you. To you, Christine (from book club) for all the kindness and love you showed me in the early days of my writing. You have my love. Steve Singh for allowing me to network back in the day and for being a true friend. The

Legatus Law team for their support especially during the days leading up to the completion of the book! Carole and Mike for the all round continuous love and support. To a friend who helped me explore internal networking. To everyone that inspired me and encouraged me to network even when the going was tough. Finally, thanks to Portugal for giving me the space to work.

A very heartfelt thanks to those that I interviewed: Gareth Boot, Eddie Davies, Leo de Montaignac, Calvin Dexter, Tracy Fletcher, Andrew Jackson, Amanda Lennon, Geoff Shepherd, and Griselda Tobogo. Your time and assistance is greatly appreciated.

Special thanks to:

Hilltop Communications for editing this book, Rushfirth Creative for the illustrations and Becky Gorman of Becky Joy Photography for the cover image.

Your notes on networking

21842775R00082

Printed in Great Britain
by Amazon